Alpha Dog

Alpha Dog

Leading, Managing, and Motivating in the Construction Industry

MARK BRESLIN

McALLY
INTERNATIONAL
PRESS

© 2010 Mark Breslin. Printed and bound in the United States of America. All rights reserved. No part of this book may be reproduced or transmitted in any form or by any means, electronic or mechanical, including photocopying, recording, or by an information storage and retrieval system—except by a reviewer who may quote brief passages in a review to be printed in a magazine, newspaper, or on the Web—without permission in writing from the publisher. For information, please contact McAlly International Press, 7172 Regional Street #430, Dublin, CA 94568.

Although the author and publisher have made every effort to ensure the accuracy and completeness of information contained in this book, we assume no responsibility for errors, inaccuracies, omissions, or any inconsistency herein. Any slighting of people, places, or organizations is unintentional.

First printing 2010
Second printing 2010

ISBN 978-0-9741662-8-5
LCCN 2009933864

ATTENTION CORPORATIONS, UNIVERSITIES, COLLEGES, AND PROFESSIONAL ORGANIZATIONS: Quantity discounts are available on bulk purchases of this book for educational, gift purposes, or as premiums for increasing magazine subscriptions or renewals. Special books or book excerpts can also be created to fit specific needs. For information, please contact McAlly International Press, 7172 Regional Street #430, Dublin, CA 94568; 925-705-7662; jdixon@breslin.biz; www.breslin.biz.

Dedication

To Mom and Bob
who showed me the way.

A Native American elder was asked how he handled his own inner struggles about his abilities and achieving his intentions for himself and his people.

He replied: "Inside of me there are two dogs. One of the dogs is unhappy, insecure, and full of doubt. He is harsh and negative and quick with criticism. The other dog is joyful and confident. He is supportive and playful. The doubtful dog fights the confident dog all the time."

When asked which dog wins, he reflected for a moment and replied, "The one I feed the most."

Contents

Introduction

*"If I have seen farther than others it is because
I was standing on the shoulders of giants."*
—SIR ISAAC NEWTON

I write this book on the shoulders of giants. On the shoulders of three generations of my family in construction before me. On the shoulders of my mentors and guides. On the shoulders of every guy who ever gave me a piece of advice or a kind word. On those of CEOs of billion-dollar contracting firms and an old wise field guy who could neither read nor write. I have been privileged to stand on the shoulders of construction giants for my entire life, and what I have seen and learned I now want to share. It is truly my purpose and privilege to help you to succeed.

There is no business as interesting, challenging, and provoking as construction. In twenty-five years on the frontlines of this business I have been schooled by some of the most remarkable leaders in North America. These people are hard-driving, visionary, and concerned only with who you are and what you can do. I have dedicated my professional life to this industry because I cannot imagine working with anyone else. I would never have fit in anyplace else.

There are no new revelations in this book. It is not some great work of enlightening business strategy. It probably does not cover everything it should. But it does contain a lot of what a construction leader needs to know, and it's information not taught in college courses on construction management or engineering. It's not taught in apprenticeship programs either. Foremen are the self-taught heroes of our business, but no one ever gave them tools like these to reach their potential.

It is up to each individual reader to gain what you can from this effort. I fall short in my own eyes, for I am still an Alpha Dog in development. I'm more than two decades at the grindstone, and yet I still have areas to polish. But that's what I love about this industry; you can still be who you are (even a little rough around the edges) on the way up. It will be to my great satisfaction if everyone from apprentices to top leaders can use this material to improve their abilities to lead our industry into the future.

Finally, I would like to thank the hundreds of thousands of people who have now read my books, attended my speeches, and shared my passion for this industry. Those who know me realize I don't bullshit around, and I'm pretty sure this book's tone and content live up to that standard of truth. Though I promote a leadership ethic based on self-knowledge, sincerity, and integrity, don't underestimate the uncompromising nature of my overall message. If you want to be an Alpha Dog, you must find within yourself a backbone of steel, a relentless commitment, and a greater vision of yourself. Life is too short to be anything less than what you are capable of being, and that is how I've tried to live my own life so far. I hope this book and the lessons you learn from your giants will also inspire you to realize a greater vision of yourself and accomplish remarkable things at work and in life.

—MARK BRESLIN

CHAPTER ONE

Alpha Dog

The Rewards of "Willing to Try"

The bull lowers his head and charges. I try to dodge, but it's too late. Somewhere people are happy and carefree. Somewhere people are living lives free of risk and stress. But in the Pamplona bullring these people are far, far away...as more than a thousand pounds of angry bull slams into me and begins pile-driving me into the ground.

Construction is a business that rewards boldness. In order to be successful one must take on higher and higher levels of risk. It's all about "going for it." It's about pushing your own limits and those of others. It is voluntary. It is scary. It is challenging. It is addictive. It is the story of the Alpha.

The Running of the Bulls occurs in Pamplona, Spain, each year. For the last four hundred years for eight days in July, starting at 8 A.M., two thousand men and twelve bulls run. The bulls weigh 1,700 lbs. and have razor-sharp horns. They are not happy. Twelve-foot-high barricades keep the bulls and runners in the street. The Spaniards will push you back over these fences if you lose your nerve and try to get out. Eight hundred first-aid personnel are on the course. Local papers have box scores with the daily number of injuries and hospitalizations. I am standing inside the barricades. It is 7:59.

The risk one is willing to accept to become an Alpha depends upon the opportunity sought. The elements influencing the decision include environment, skills, opportunities, and rewards. Our industry generally drives Alpha opportunity and performance to the absolute edge. And the absolute edge is where the greatest rewards can be found; but it's not always an easy place to go.

I should have listened to Alfredo. He met us at the hotel reception, eyeing the gringos in our white-and-red clothes. "Señor Breslin, you come to run with the bulls, no?" "Yes," I replied. "This is a bad thing," he said gravely. "Many people die. Many hurt bad-

ly. These bulls have been bred for hundreds of years to be killers. I say, do not do this thing."

There are some things in life you do just because you want to see what they feel like. There are some things in life that look pretty intimidating when you first think about them. There are some things in life that bring out those who really want to test their limits. And there is nothing like the feeling out at the limit. There is nothing like being around those who share a bold and unlimited view of themselves. Adventurous. Relentless. Ambitious. Brothers-in-arms.

Eight o'clock. The rocket is fired. The roar of the crowd deafens. We jog at first. Then, suddenly, everyone takes off. In a full sprint everything is a blur. Jumping over fallen runners with their hands over their heads, I look over my shoulder. The bulls are bearing down on us. We run through the stadium tunnel and into the bullring. Here comes the stampede. In the ring bulls zigzag wildly through the runners. They scrape the side rail, and dozens of runners dive up into the seats. I turn to look, but it's too late. The bull lowers his head. Slow motion impact. I am knocked into the air. Now I'm sprawled in the arena dirt. I roll over to see a giant black frothing face bearing down upon me. I reach up and grab a horn.

Accepting personal challenge and risk creates momentum, focus, and pressure to perform. In the midst of the greatest challenges people and organizations are measured by their responses. And as wild as the ride may be, there is often something really fun and fulfilling on the other side. You have to get out there and try, though, or you'll never know what might have been.

I am dragged and bounced across the ring. I hold that horn for dear life. Finally, a dozen other local runners drive the bull off. I lie in the dirt with a circle of faces looking down. Slowly, they lift me up, clothes filthy, camera smashed, dazed, bloody, and bruised. Slowly, twenty-five thousand bullring spectators rise to roar their approval. I raise my hands above my head, glad to be alive. It is quite a moment. A simple reward for being willing to try.

The Alpha

Definition of "Alpha": (1) The first letter of the Greek alphabet; (2) the first or the beginning; (3) the brightest or main star in a constellation; (4) being the highest ranked or most dominant.

I am not inventing something new with the title of this book or the concept of the Alpha. Nature has had a million years to work on the concept. She has it worked out pretty well. All biology, animal life, propagation, and the best shows on *Animal Planet* display the influence and importance of Alpha behavior and identity. Alpha leadership is part of nature's plan to keep us safe and healthy. From the birds and bees to everything that lives and breathes, the Alpha concept of leader behavior is on display. Just because you wear clothes and claim to be a higher form of life does not make you immune to the dynamics nature has been working out over millions of years. Everywhere you turn, top leadership defines outcomes in our lives.

In our homes. At our churches. In our workplaces. In social clubs. On sports teams. In governance of our towns, states, and country. Everywhere, all the time, there are leaders and followers. And it has been that way since the beginning of time. It is leaders who have determined the direction and outcome of every form of human organization and every bit of history. Alphas have always made the greatest impact and difference. Through leadership all that is possible occurs. Through leadership the progress of man, society, technology, art, sport, and every other endeavor is determined.

And since the beginning of time people just like you and me have looked at the Alpha leader role and asked themselves one question: "Why not me?"

Why Not You?

Why shouldn't you seek a greater leadership role now and in the future?

Many people who ask themselves that question are capable of remarkable things yet are not brave enough to try. They have the desire to lead but lack the self-knowledge, confidence, and/or skills to change or to risk failure. If the first seeds of desire do not actually take root as initiative, one's Alpha potential withers and dies.

For many, especially in this industry, the question of whether *I* am fit to lead is asked many times over a career. No matter if you are just starting out or seeking to improve your position or even looking down from the very top of the construction industry's leadership elite, it is likely you have been asking yourself this question. And most importantly you must ask yourself that question honestly: Why not me? And if not, why not?

Are You the Obstacle?

Someone is going to lead at every level of the organizations you work for over the lifetime of your employment. So the choice is very simple: It will either be you or someone else. The first person to object to it being you may be someone you don't know as well as you think you do. That person is you.

The biggest obstacle to embracing leadership roles tends to be people's limited views of themselves and their potential. What thoughts or feelings might hold people back from taking on leadership challenges during their careers?

- I don't have the confidence.
- I've never done it before.
- No one asked me to.
- I don't have the right education or degree.

- I don't want the headache.
- I'd rather complain about the boss than be one.
- I'm not smart enough.
- I'm not sure I'd like it.
- I don't want to fail.
- I'm not experienced enough.
- I can't handle conflict.
- I'm not old enough.
- I couldn't handle the responsibility.
- _____ [fill in name] is better than I am.
- I tried leading once [kickball, third grade] and failed.

Take your pick. They are all readily available excuses. And if you ride that excuse long enough, someone else will be your leader, boss, superintendent, or foreman for the next year, decade, or even your entire career.

When trying to make the decision to advance, don't expect the answer to hit you like lightning. The skies are not going to open. Some deep voice is not going to tell you that you are a "chosen one." It is more likely just the opposite. You will have to think about whether it works for you. The question of "Why not you?" does not need to be answered at this very moment. Just don't give a permanent answer that limits your potential or ambition without at least a thoughtful interval.

Remember, though, that most everyone has doubts about their abilities. Self-doubt is something you will most always find with leaders. Many of the most successful people I know are driven by fear of failure. They may hide it well, but it is the driving force of their success. The difference between them and you is that they embraced the opportunity and kept moving up. They faced down their insecurities, fears, and doubts. They took action instead of letting those negative voices in their heads freeze them where they were.

Take the time to answer the leadership question thoughtfully. Leadership opportunities will still be waiting if you don't take too long to decide. What do these opportunities look like?

The Construction Alpha Opportunity

If the Alpha challenge is for you, and you have overcome your obstacles, I truly congratulate you. I also have some excellent news for you. If you embrace leadership in the construction industry over the next ten to fifteen years, an unprecedented opportunity is waiting for you.

The demographic and generational shifts occurring in our population are going to change the leadership dynamic in every organization in the U.S. and Canada. They will impact every employee within those organizations, including you. Just consider some of the following numbers:

Generations in the Workplace		
Traditionals	70,000,000	born before 1946
Baby Boomers	80,000,000	born between 1946 and 1964
Generation X	46,000,000	born between 1965 and 1981
Generation Y	78,000,000	born between 1982 and 2000

There are four generations noted in this chart, and the interrelationship among them is what is going to create the greatest leadership opportunity in the history of the U.S. and Canada. What the chart above really tells is the coming story of generational leadership change.

As you will note, the first generation is the Traditionalists. These are people who were born before 1946. These were likely your parents or grandparents. Many if not most of this population segment have already exited the workforce or gone into semi-retirement.

The Traditionals' kids were mostly part of the Baby Boomer generation. As you will note, it includes more than eighty million people born between 1946 and 1964. They constitute the majority of the workforce in all industries in North America today. Why is this significant relative to construction leadership challenges and opportunities? The Baby Boomers are going into their retirement cycle. If you examine this trend, you will see that within a short time period the Baby Boomers will be leaving the industry to new generations of workers and leaders. Most importantly, in terms of industry leadership, the majority of all Boomer foremen, superintendents, and lead workers will soon be moving toward retirement.

Tens of thousands of construction management and supervisory positions will be opening up each year, all at the same time. Think about it for a second. Who runs or manages nearly all of your organization's personnel or programs in the office and field? Boomers actually run the entire construction industry, and they are on their way out. So these advancement opportunities will exist all up and down the chain of command. It doesn't matter whether you are an apprentice or a CEO, you need to be planning ahead. Look at the following illustration for an example.

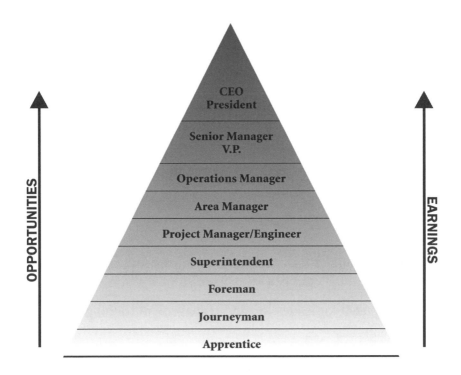

As you see, there is unlimited upward mobility in the construction industry. This goes for both positions and financial rewards. The career plan of any ambitious person in the industry should be to keep moving up. For the next fifteen years or more there will be a real opportunity for upward mobility.

Thus, the unprecedented opportunity and challenge is the replacement of all these retiring Boomers with new Generation X and Generation Y leaders. These young people will have an incredible opportunity to manage and lead at an earlier stage of their careers than their parents or any other previous generation. This is great news for them, but what does it mean for the entire industry? Along with the remarkable opportunities, what are some of the challenges of construction leadership transition in this same time period?

- The challenge of recruitment, development, and overall replacement of more than fifty percent of top leaders, managers, foremen, and key employees

- Significant shortages and competition for top leadership candidates
- Unseasoned younger people thrust into positions they may not be ready to handle
- The necessity of organizational mentoring programs being rapidly developed and launched
- Many more rookie field employees also being managed by less experienced leaders
- Increasing loss of organizational experience and intellectual capital
- Different generational expectations, norms, and communication styles, leading to conflict
- A huge need for leadership and management training programs and materials

What does this mean for a reader of this book? Well, it depends on what generation you are in and how you look at leadership and its impact on you in the workplace. No matter what generation you are in, here are some of the functional uses of the strategies within this book:

- As a tool for existing leaders to improve their performance and professionalism
- As a tool for mentoring new leaders toward independence and success
- To provide clear lessons for existing leaders to improve jobsite outcomes
- To set standards and expectations for prospective leaders, whether they work in the office or the field
- To inspire and empower promising apprentices, journeymen, project managers, and engineers

- To serve as training materials for contractors, associations, union apprentice instructors, professors, JATC coordinators, and training directors

The Construction Alpha opportunity is real. Don't say nobody told you.

Examining Your "Why"

Assuming this opportunity is so great, why might you want to be a leader? There has to be an underlying motivation for anyone to seek leadership advancement. Some reasons are noble and remarkable. Some reasons are selfish or self-serving. Here is a short list of possible motivators:

- Power
- Money
- Recognition
- Prestige and image
- Ability to make a difference
- A desire to change people or organizations
- Don't like being told what to do
- Self-esteem
- Competitive achievement
- An opportunity to see one's own ideas in action
- Self-centered nature
- Need to dominate or control
- Challenge and self-development

To be a good leader, you really have to understand your own "why" because it will be reflected in everything you do. From motivating others to personal ethics, it will define your leadership style. At the minimum you need to ask yourself, why do I want the responsibility of leadership? This self-awareness is a critical window to your own fundamental motivations because at a basic level of human insight, if you can't understand what motivates and drives you, then you sure as hell shouldn't be in charge of others. A leader without the capacity of self-reflection will never be much good to anyone.

Leader of the Pack: By Invitation Only

You must also understand that whatever you do to develop yourself into an Alpha leader, 95 percent of the time someone else will decide if and when you are ready. It doesn't matter what you think about you; leadership is by invitation only. By promotion, election, or assignment, you will reach leadership when others elevate you. Leadership is an opportunity others provide you with because of your talent, value, or capacity. By-invitation-only leadership has a few problems, though. If you want to move up and others don't notice you, your ability or desire can be missed. On the other hand, if someone knows how to "get the invitation" or "work the angles" through charisma or connections, he or she may be elevated above others who would perform much better. This is just a reality check for you to think about. If you want to rise up, others must know that you desire it, or you may be passed over. Leadership is not about being silently humble, waiting for someone to ask you. It is about starting as early as possible in developing yourself and conveying your interest so others have the opportunity to determine whether you are the right person in the right place at the right time.

You Can Lead from Anywhere

Some readers are probably thinking, "I'm just an apprentice. Or I'm just a journeyman. Nobody listens to me. How can I lead?" This book is based on the premise that you can lead from anywhere. If you are already a senior manager, your role is obvious. But what about those "regular guys"? What about recent graduates of apprentice or college programs? What about green recruits or the lowest man on the totem pole? Yes, you can lead from there as well. Consider yourself, from this moment on (no matter where you are in your job or organization), a leader in training. There is no perfect standard for when someone arrives as a leader.

Leading from anywhere is behavior driven. It starts with the embracing of responsibility. As often as possible. This leads to a contribution to decision making. Whenever anyone will listen. And then finally the taking of initiative. You have to show through your actions that you're a leader in training, ready to move up. These steps are what enable you to lead from anywhere. No one is going to call out your name. No one is going to hand you the secret. No education or degree automatically qualifies you. And though you may not always feel empowered or entitled or may not think you have the tools, skills, confidence, or background…none of that matters. The only thing that matters is that you embrace leadership behaviors from this very moment forward. Doing so requires courage, honesty, humility, and action. Don't forget that leading from anywhere starts with learning from anywhere.

There are going to be people who will challenge the idea of your leading from anywhere. Your peers may resent you. "Who does he think he is anyway?" Your friends may second-guess you. "He is not any better than us; what makes him think he can be or do more?" Your immediate supervisor may be threatened. But, honestly, there is only one person you really have to watch out for. There is only one person whose opinion can destroy your future prospects and leadership quest. And as we noted before, that person is you.

CHAPTER TWO

The Mirror

"Before you are a leader, success is all about growing yourself. When you become a leader, success is all about growing others."
—JACK WELCH

A Man of Self-Knowledge and Purpose

We are thirty-five miles off the tip of Baja, fishing on the Tropic of Cancer, where the swells roll three thousand miles from Hawaii and marlin rule as fearless kings of the sea. Upon this vast and unforgiving ocean, I prepare for battle. In anticipation of the adrenaline and a marlin hitting at 75 mph, I am in the hands of our captain, a man following his destiny, a man of self-knowledge and purpose.

How do we know what we're doing with our lives is worthy and purposeful? It is not something most of us think much about. We often just do what we do (or what we've always done) without reflection. To some degree our actions speak for us in this regard. A life aligned with purpose and self-knowledge is reflected in the consistency of someone's values and actions. They are not only very successful, well-respected, and "real people" in the best sense of the words but fulfilled for having found truth in the expression of their lives. It is easy to settle for less. In much the same way, a business reflects the driving purpose of its leaders in its values, actions, and achievements. A man or woman's purpose is a compass and the foundation upon which one builds not only a successful business but a life of meaning and reward. But you've got to know who you are.

Enrique Vega was born a captain's son. His father, reduced to yellowed Cabo newspaper clips, was an unequaled master of 1,000 lb. marlins and six-hour fights to the death. Now it's Enrique's time to be more than his father's son. Mid-forties, short and stocky, sporting a tattered shirt and weathered face. No sign of expression.

His eyes, behind black shades, relentlessly search the deep blue wa-
ters. On the flying bridge, he rocks barefoot, in perfect unison with
the pounding swells, breaking wave after countless wave.

To know one's purpose takes some searching, but life is too short not to face the challenge. For the individual it may mean stirring deep waters or crossing dark storms of doubt. For a business it is more like boiling something down to its bare essence. Many of us understand the benefit of this quest for personal or business align-ment but are unwilling to try. Too many substitutes can be found to excuse us from self-evaluation, honesty, and change. Without bru-tally honest self-examination, it is easy to drift in the currents of fate rather than face necessary changes of course. Looking within, with continuous discipline and a focus on the compass, is the true test of business and self-mastery.

He talked without ego or pride. Of braving storms with thir-
ty-foot swells, of epic battles and dangerous encounters, won and
lost. All the while, as if unconscious of the effort, his scarred and
callused hands worked the throttle and wheel in perfect symmetry
to invisible currents. I asked him how often he was offshore fish-
ing on the ocean. In his halting English he responded, "Depending
on weather, maybe 330 days a year...for the last fifteen years." I
looked at the horizon...and tried to imagine five thousand days at
the helm.

Each of us faces the same challenges of alignment and purpose. Tens of thousands of companies, hundreds of thousands of foremen's efforts, and billions of dollars ride on the outcomes of our efforts ev-ery day. And to succeed, as should an individual or business owner, we must turn inward for our answers, to examine our purpose and our actions again and again in the service of improvement. Business success depends on a powerful formula based on self-evaluation, honesty, and willingness to change. The ultimate success and fulfill-ment of potential, of an individual or business, will be a reflection of the alignment of action with purpose. But to know your purpose, you must know yourself.

"Only thirty days off each year?" I asked, "What do you do on those days?" He slowly turned and took off his shades. Serious, dark, and clear, his eyes burned with passion. "First, I clean my boat perfect. Then I change the oil and check the motors... then I go sixty miles offshore...and out there I go for the big blue marlin...alone."

Minutes later my line and reel screamed.... I strapped into the fighting chair...and tensed every muscle to set the hook. As I cranked the reel, an eight-foot marlin leaped and thrashed the water two hundred yards aft. I looked over at Enrique. He was smiling.

A Hard Look in the Mirror

How many times a day do you look into a mirror? At least once or twice I would think. Why do you do it? Well, here might be a few reasons:

- To check how you look before going out
- To see if you have something large and green in your teeth
- To admire your appearance (pump that bicep)
- To critique your flaws (suck in that gut)
- To see how you appear to the world

Over the course of a year you probably look into a mirror three to five hundred times. You don't even think about it; you just do it as a part of life. But for all those times you do it, you are only checking one thing: your external looks.

What about the internal you? Where is your mirror for that check-in? Where, when, and how do you look at yourself for who you are and not what you look like? The value of looking into a mirror that reveals who we really are is critical for anyone who wants to be successful. Being a good leader starts with knowing yourself. It requires self-examination. It requires self-honesty. It requires a hard look in the mirror.

Imagine taking the time to honestly look at yourself—your motivations, beliefs, fears, behaviors, relationships, accomplishments, and failures—three to five hundred times a year. Besides being exhausting, it would surely be enlightening. Why? Because it would help you see yourself the way you really are. It might even promote positive change.

On the other hand, imagine for a second that you removed all the mirrors from your home, that you never looked in a mirror to see how you looked. What would be the result? You probably would let your appearance decline. You'd probably look a lot less presentable to the world. Others would notice. It might be a bad thing.

That is precisely my point. If you don't look into your internal mirror, the same thing happens. If you're not examining yourself, then you are just hoping that the reflection of who you really are is good enough. A leader cannot afford to be that blind. Before leaders can be responsible for others, they must know themselves. And there is only one way to get there—a hard look in the mirror to cultivate self-knowledge.

Self-Knowledge: Your Alpha Foundation

Self-knowledge and management are the foundations for successful long-term leadership capability. You have to look at leadership as a long-term personal and professional evolution rather than a one-time event (promotion). Self-knowledge (the mirror) is a tool to be used for this evolution. Self-knowledge includes understanding the following:

- What are my main motivations?
- What are my strongest skill sets, and where do I need assistance?
- Do I lead from strategy or emotion?
- What are my main strengths in dealing with people?
- Do I make decisions from instinct or logic?
- Am I a reactive person or a proactive person?
- What is my "gift" as a person that makes me remarkable, and how does it impact those around me?
- What is my fatal flaw and how does it impact people around me?
- What level of intuition do I bring to motivating others?
- Can I take brutally honest feedback in service of my advancement?
- Am I secure enough in myself to lead well?
- How do I generally behave under extreme stress?

I have seen prospective leaders fall short of their potential because they simply could not be honest with themselves. They were unwilling to dig into the challenge of self-knowledge. And that is understandable. We often find more things we don't like about ourselves when we do it, which is precisely why we need to do it. The polite term is self-deception. The true description is bullshitting yourself.

Friends, Family, and Coworkers Are Not Your Mirror

In the absence of the hard look in the mirror, we tend to use others as our reflection of our ability, worth, or potential. We are unduly influenced by others' opinions rather than our own insights. And those whom we are around the most have the most influence on us in that regard. Who are we around most? Friends, family and coworkers.

Perhaps you are one of the very lucky people in life whose family, friends, and coworkers are totally supportive, non-judgmental, and highly objective. They are wise, insightful, and honest with themselves and you. They don't let their relationship with you cloud their ability to advise or admire you. If you have this going on, then you are one of the rare ones because often family and friends are just too close to you to help you.

When looking for ways to advance yourself, you are probably going to have to go outside your trusted circle of family and friends. They are simply too close to be objective. Your coworkers will often have an axe to grind about your advancement. They may like and admire you, but their view will be impacted by your prospective advancement. You are going to need to find people you admire. You are going to need to find role models who have what you need. You have to find people who are going to challenge you through blunt honesty and professional accountability.

Friends and family cannot always serve this role. There are too many filters involved, too many personal emotions, and too much history. There are too many roles that get in the way: father, daughter, son, best friend, and all the expectations that come with these roles. If I really believed my mom that "I'm special just because I'm me," that doesn't leave a lot of room for my improvement.

Don't misunderstand me. Family and friends offer us love, security, and trust. Loyalty and connectivity are the ties that bind. Unfortunately, often our families and friends are too close, too negative, or too judgmental to bring real objective value to our professional development. They are not your mirror; you are. Do not allow them or anyone else to reflect back anything but the truth of your potential.

You Are Not Perfect (or Batting 1.000)

You don't look in the mirror just once when trying to decide if you are going to be a leader. You have to check it all the time. Sometimes, once people have gained in confidence or moved up the construction chain of command, they think they no longer need to examine themselves. This can be a serious mistake, so let me help you see things more clearly.

Those of you already in management positions are not as good leaders as you think you are. Your employees don't like you as much as you think they do. Your team does not admire you like you believe they do. Your mistakes are more visible than you think they are. Your personality is not as winning as you would like. You are not perfect. You are not batting 1.000.

Like driving your car or trying to check your bald spot, there are places that you just can't see. And you probably don't want to. Personal blind spots are easier to ignore than accept. One important part of your evolution as a leader and manager is not waiting for these blind spots to smack you in the face. Pretending something is really not you or your problem until it shows up on your jobsite or in your workplace is not the way to go. It might be the easy way, but the clean-up on that can be a problem. Instead, it is about being brutally honest with yourself so that you can continue to grow as a manager, leader, and person.

We find it hard to recognize or accept that we are not as good as we want to be or need to be. Well, here is the good news: Failure is inevitable. To get into the Baseball Hall of Fame, you only need to bat near .320 for a career. That means you only have to succeed three or four out of ten times. It means that to be among the most successful in the game you must accept that you will fail more than you succeed. And this failure has to serve as the means for improvement, focus, and re-dedication.

You have to accept that you are not and never will be as good as you can be as a manager or leader or person. As soon as you accept that without doubting yourself or becoming defensive, you are in the right mindset to lead.

Business Blind Spots (Mine)

On the subject of blind spots I would like to share some painful lessons I learned. After my first few years of top leadership I thought I was gold. I led organizational growth. Great finances. New initiatives. Strong momentum. So around this time I had a major contractor I had known for eight years come into my office and close the door. Now, here was a guy who had smiled at me and shook my hand for almost a decade. We had just finished working on a very intense project together, and I thought he was coming in to offer me praise for a job well done. Instead, he hit me across the head with a two-by-four.

"Mark, you do a really good job," he said, "but you know, for all these eight years before I really got to work with you, I didn't like you. I've been thinking what everyone else in the industry thinks. I know it's hard to hear, but everyone thinks that you are a real asshole. But as it turns out, you're a pretty good guy." Ouch. What a gut punch. What a blind spot.

What this very stand-up guy was trying to tell me was that my personal style was abrasive and non-cooperative, that I hadn't looked in the mirror and that it was a problem for me and my organization. In the process of trying to get the job done, I had left a lot of dead bodies behind. And worst of all, I didn't even know it. I thought that results came before people, and as a young leader full of ambition, I simply did not pay enough attention to how I was coming across. No one had questioned my loyalty, talent, commitment, or drive. With all those results I figured I was succeeding.

What I learned was that my opinion of myself doesn't matter if I'm not living up to my potential as a leader of people. But since I was an arrogant little a-hole, I promptly forgot about the conversation and went back to doing all the same things. Until a few months later.

One of my bright and talented employees came to me to tell me she was going to resign and move to Japan to teach English. I was happy for her and asked to do an exit interview on her last day. On that day I asked her about her training, our work environment, the tools and technology we provided. My last question to her was, "So, what was it like working for me?" She did not hesitate for a second. She looked me in the eye and told me, "Mark, in three years of working for you, not one day was enjoyable." Sheee-it. *Tell me how you really feel....* Blind spot identified. Mark got the message. No place to hide. Problem needs attention now.

Pay close attention to the feedback you get from your most honest peers or employees. Try to look at yourself in the most objective manner that you can on an ongoing basis. Ask for direct input on your blind spots (but don't get defensive when people give you truthful answers). The answers these people gave me became catalysts for my personal change as a leader. Blind spots—everybody's got them, but only a fraction of good leaders and managers are willing to take them on.

Don't Be Defensive

Be prepared for the discomfort of the truth. The honest input you ask for very well may reflect an ugly mug. People you ask may give you answers that really piss you off. How will you handle it? Defensiveness is a natural reaction to criticism. But after the two shocks noted above I learned a valuable lesson. Now, I love criticism. I cannot get enough of it. Want to give me an "atta-boy"? Keep it. Want to give me a "You're doing great"? Fine—that and a cup of coffee gets me through another five minutes. I never learned a thing from someone's praise. The best thing someone can do is give me honest and non-judgmental criticism of my ideas or performance. Challenge me or chew my ass off with some sincerity and love, and I am a happy man. This is because it is a tool for me to grow.

Why do I need this tool? I mean, let's be honest. Who am I to judge myself? I am the worst person to judge myself. You are probably the worst person to judge yourself. We generally cannot or will not see ourselves accurately and objectively. So, we should welcome every possible opportunity to up our game by getting good feedback and criticism.

Now, that all sounds nice, but the reality is that the first reaction you will have to any form of criticism is defensiveness. And it is only about a three-second fuse that will take you from "Thanks for the feedback" to "F-U, Mr. Know-it-All." But that is your self-protection getting in the way of your personal growth. Defensiveness is a barrier to improvement. Defensiveness is often a reaction to the truth. Try to suck it up and love it. If you always play defense, it can become a part of your organizational culture. If your team members see you being reluctant to accept accurate or honest criticism, how do you think they are going to model their own behaviors when you try to be blunt and yet constructively honest with them? Don't be defensive.

BYOB: Bring Your Own Best

Usually, when we look at ourselves, we quickly see the things we don't like. Physical, mental, or emotional—it's easy to identify those things we wish we could change. But just as importantly we need to take stock of the positive attributes we bring to others' lives. These very well may be the pillars upon which your leadership rests. But you have to recognize, acknowledge, and own them.

BYOB = Bring Your Own Best. What exactly is that for you, and how does it contribute to your ability to lead well? Take a moment and write down five positive words you believe really define yourself.

1. _____

2. _____

3. _____

4. _____

5. _____

Did you find that difficult? Most people do. But the words you wrote above are the BYOB that you stand upon as the starting place of your leadership. These temper the problem areas that need attention or improvement. You cannot count on these alone to carry you, but neither should you forget the power of them when well applied. And if you couldn't fill in those five lines, you are either too modest, out of touch with yourself, or a total negative loser who should never lead anyone.

If You Need Love or Approval, Do Not Apply

Being an Alpha requires a tough-minded approach to work, people, and challenges. Therefore, if your mirror reflects a strong need to be liked all the time, it is going to be very difficult to advance. Being tough-minded does not mean acting in an offensive manner. It means you have to deal with things in a very straightforward way. It often requires you to put outcomes ahead of everyone's approval. Leaders frequently find it lonely when their decisions are not universally liked. In fact, most leaders recognize that a certain number of people will not agree with them or even actively dislike them, and yet they are not influenced by that fact. They know the leader's job is to earn and command respect. Being liked or approved of is just a bonus.

CHAPTER THREE

Alpha Leader

"Never tell people how to do things. Tell them what to do and they will surprise you with their ingenuity."

—GENERAL GEORGE S. PATTON

Lead Change or Others Will

(All these examples actually occurred.)

My kindergarten girlfriend told me she just had to move on.... Playing Superman, I ran right through the sliding glass patio door.... I bounced around the back seat as the car rolled then hit the tree head-on....

If you want to lead, you cannot refuse to adapt. Change happens whether we like it or not. Sometimes we try to refuse it anyway. We wait. We stall. To our own detriment. Our ability to accept change in life and business circumstances most often determines our path. The immediacy of our response is a reflection of a million years of instinctual capacity to quickly adapt to events and learn from them.

...the full five-gallon can of gas ignited right next to me... your dog is lost...yours is the first case in the western hemisphere in ten years...the engine burst into flames as we rolled out the doors.... Mark, now you're the boss....

In construction this same instinctual capacity to accept change and rapidly adapt is something that leaders must utilize. When problems and challenges occur, there is sometimes a tendency to remain in denial for a period. Or other times we simply solve the problem of the moment and move on—the reality of the situation not accepted, the change lesson lost. Neither one of these outcomes works in construction. Remember the parable "Give a man a fish, he eats for a day; teach a man to fish, he eats for a lifetime"? Changes, challenges, and problems provide the chance to learn and then to teach others to fish. Over time, these opportunities create individuals and teams that anticipate, accept, and adapt to change.

I slid down to the edge of the cliff and froze…the undertow sucked me out beyond the breakers…the street person's eyes bulged as he pointed the gun at me…my horse started bucking wildly…the dog ate an entire sweat sock.…

Those who accept and promote change will be the leaders of the future. This applies to everyone, including foremen, superintendents, project managers, and CEOs. It's no joke. "Back-in-the-day" thinking is no longer an option; for leadership, adaptability is a mandatory mindset and business strategy. Technology, employee trends, tools and materials, management strategies, market shifts—you name it, it is all changing. And changing faster and faster. It is Alpha Go or No Go. For a more profitable business, for more motivated and fulfilled employees, for an upward path of leadership, for any prospective Alpha, acceptance of change and rapid adaptation is the path.

We called in help on the SAT phone…two hundred CEOs waited for my next line.…

What or who needs to change in your life or in your business? Lead change or others will. Choose.

First Things First

The Alpha Dog vs. The Born Leader

The construction industry is full of hard-working, hard-driving personalities. And this is how most leaders are chosen. Construction rewards aggressive, determined go-getters who by force of will seem to shine as "born leaders." But this is a mistake that costs the construction industry billions of dollars in lost opportunities every year. Let me explain why.

"Born leaders" are identified by their characteristics. An assumption about their capabilities is made based on innate traits: personality, presentation, or profile. Alleged born leaders are usually identified by things such as:

- Dominant personality
- Charismatic or magnetic nature
- Driving and determined nature
- Kick-ass work ethic
- Hard and skilled worker
- Aggressive go-getter
- Competitive spirit
- Dynamic communicator

And these things are why they are selected and promoted. The best guy in the crowd who has these characteristics is chosen from the pack and given leader status. The problem is that quite often in the industry that's where the process ends. "Born leaders" must execute their responsibilities with nothing more than what got them selected. What they really need is ongoing training and tools to become a professional leader and manager. A so-called born leader without these tools is stuck trying to do the best they can with what they've got.

Here is my take on that approach:

- I don't want a "born doctor" working on my kid.
- I don't want a "born mechanic" working on my car.
- I don't want a "born CPA" doing my taxes.
- I don't want a "born dentist" drilling my teeth.
- And I don't want a "born leader" running my construction project or organization.

Leaders are made and refined by training and experience. Unfortunately, when an organization or individual has a belief system that supports the "born-leader" approach, several consequences result:

- Training to professionalize construction leadership and management is marginalized or not provided.
- New leaders and managers are not given the tools to succeed.
- Quieter prospects for leadership are overlooked.
- Those aspiring to lead compare themselves to the dominant personalities and decline the opportunity.
- The performance deficiencies of "born leaders" are visible to all team members. Thus, the credibility of the company's management approach takes a big hit, and performance suffers.
- Advancement can be skewed by personality vs. competence.
- Those anointed as "born to lead" are reluctant to examine their capabilities objectively and resist the need to upgrade their skill sets. These tendencies can lead to arrogance and overconfidence.
- No one in the ranks of born leaders nor those working for them reaches his or her full potential.

The idea that leaders and Alphas are born and not made has led many in our industry to make other bad assumptions about leadership:

- Leaders are born, not made, so we can just put the most aggressive person in charge and let him or her carry it off.
- Leaders are born, not made, and since I don't see myself that way, then I must not be one.
- Born leaders are self-sufficient and independent. They don't need (or don't ask) for help.
- As a born leader my role is to tell everyone what to do (despite the fact that everyone else sees me as an arrogant hothead), whether or not I have the skills to do so.
- As a natural born leader I do not have to work on myself as a person or leader.

The point should be clear enough. Leadership starts with the character and personality of the individual. But after that, leadership is learned and then earned.

Good Leadership Basics

Good leader behavior is sometimes pretty subtle. It can be a combination of manners, style, communication, body language, and self-awareness. What is strange to me is how often I see leaders (even some very senior ones) ignore the basics. Here are some basic leader behaviors that I believe naturally indicate Alpha status to those around a person exemplifying them:

- When entering a room or coming on a jobsite, take the time to greet everyone by name.
- When someone enters a room, take time to stand and greet him or her.
- Shake hands upon arrival and departure.
- Have a firm and straightforward shake. Keep the bro shake at home.
- Greet people with a friendly manner.
- Maintain excellent eye contact at all times. For you young Alphas that means not looking at your cell phone or Blackberry every two minutes.
- Make people feel good about themselves when they are around you.
- Do not look or act distracted around others.
- Ask lots of questions instead of trying to prove you're the smartest guy in the room. Asking smart questions is better than trying to make smart comments.
- Don't go along with a crowd (or sit quietly) because you think they know better.
- Don't overreact too strongly to anything good or bad.

- Use your wit if you have one. If you don't, don't even try. If you are not sure you have one, you probably don't.
- Don't interrupt. Even if you can because you are in charge. Even if it seems you are listening to the stupidest thing you ever heard.
- Don't talk too much.
- Give praise and recognition whenever it is warranted.
- Be positive and encouraging in manner and style.

You Lead People, Not Employees

This has been a cornerstone of my leadership approach for the last twenty-five years. I have seen the best construction leaders in action, and there is always the recognition that leading people rather than employees provides the best results. Here are some principles to remember on this subject:

- If you want the best performance from your team and the individuals on it, you will treat them as people before employees. They will know the difference.
- The busier you get and the more pressure you are under, the harder it will be to remember that those working for you are people before they are employees.
- If you want to be fulfilled as a leader as you accomplish your organizational goals, you will also feel the pride of having developed people and not employees.
- It is nearly impossible to motivate an employee to achieve his or her highest ability. You have to reach people at a deeper level to get their best.
- Some of the most powerful leadership tools, including mentoring and coaching, are highly personal and interactive. They demand recognition of the person, not his or her job description or title.
- A life well lived is spent around interesting, challenging, inspiring, and aspiring people. How dull and one-dimensional to have

spent the bulk of one's waking hours, over a whole lifetime at work, with employees and coworkers only.

Embrace a Professional Appearance

Do not underestimate the power of appearance. A strong image of leadership competence should accompany the skills and characteristics. When I first started in the field, I came home with my clothes, hair, and boots absolutely filthy. I kind of liked being a guy who took a shower after work rather than before work. It gave me a tough-guy identity. And even now, many years later, I am a CEO who likes boots and jeans. When I look at my rack of ties, most days they all look like hangman's nooses. But that is my price of being an industry leader. It is what others are going to expect, and I have to meet those expectations or suffer the consequences.

Now, why should I care what I look like if I am in charge? If I'm "The Man," then I should be able to wear anything I want to. Well, I can't because people are very quick to make up their minds about us based on what they see. It is said that the average person makes up his or her mind about us in one minute. Unfair and stereotypical, but true. So if we have a poor appearance, we will be judged accordingly.

I learned this stuff the hard way. When I was in my twenties, I was promoted to a serious leadership position. I looked like a scruffy kid. Cheap-ass haircut. Weird plastic-rim glasses. A beard that looked like it ate my face. I didn't look like a pro. I didn't look like a leader. I looked like a guy going to a kegger. On top of this I only had two suits (which I hated to wear). Let's just say I had the job and none of the look. I told myself it was fine, but now, looking back, I really didn't feel comfortable having to change to meet others' expectations. I figured if I looked like a wild man and could do the job, then too bad for them.

What I very quickly found out was that a twenty-five-year-old with a Grizzly Adams beard and two suits isn't going to impress anyone. I also found out that I could not afford the leader look expected of me. (I could manage the ten-dollar haircut.) So I did what I had to. I cut my hair, trimmed the beard, and bought other people's used clothes.

I wasn't proud of it, but I went to used clothing stores and bought brand-name suits dirt cheap. This is stuff that other guys had cast off. Did I care? Not much. Did others care? You bet. I knew my youth was a credibility killer. I knew a poor appearance would hurt my reputation. So I had to swallow my pride until I could afford better. And that is the way of the world; your personal preference or pride doesn't mean shit to others. The project owners are looking for professionals. The public agencies, utilities, and plant managers are looking for professionals. The other contractors or subcontractors onsite are looking for professionals. The public will judge us and our industry as professionals or not by this same appearance criteria. On a jobsite or in an office you enhance or diminish your leadership prospects based on how you look.

So here are a few ideas on construction leader appearance:

- Even though your job may require you to get filthy dirty almost every day, don't necessarily look at that as your personal statement or identity. You can be a tough guy and pro leader even in clean Carhartts.

- Always be at least as well dressed and groomed as the most important people you have to deal with.

- Wear high-quality, clean, and well-maintained clothes at all times—no matter if you are an apprentice or the president of the company.

- Do not wear hats, clothes, or jewelry at work as a personal statement. Wear it as it might reflect on your company or profession.

- Don't expect everyone to accept piercings, earrings, lip rings, and other interesting metal works. A lot of people will judge a person unfavorably for these.

- If you have tattoos (like I do) consider where and when to display them.

With four generations of construction in my family I know this whole message is a tough sell. The industry is jeans and boots. Dirt and diesel. Paint and plaster. Concrete and solder and grease. Construction is not some shiny cubicle industry, but a professional can strike a balance between the two.

All Eyes Are on You

If you are a leader or want to be one, remember that even beyond your appearance, everyone is always watching you. Every minute of every day they are watching you for their cues. They are learning what is acceptable or not. They are noticing any differences between your words and deeds. Therefore, make sure that you lead by example. Make sure there is no disconnect between how you lead yourself and others. Some people think that because they are the boss they get an occasional pass. They can leverage their power or authority to deviate from the highest standards from time to time. Not even. In fact, it is totally the opposite. You have a much higher standard of performance to meet all the time. Your team will not cue you to this. In fact, you can get lulled into a false sense of security because everything seems to be "fine." But just because your team is pleasant to you does not mean they respect you and the job you are doing. You are being evaluated every day. What you did great last week might as well have been a hundred years ago. Drop the ball once, and that will be remembered for a long time. Do something right fifty times, and it is forgotten almost immediately. Unfair? You bet. A lot to live up to? Always. But your visible consistency is the virtue that allows others to trust your leadership.

You (Really) Are Man's Best Friend

As a final word to this section let's provide a salute to the Alpha man's faithful and trusty companion. Much to everyone's surprise, you, as the tough Alpha (really) are every man's (and woman's) best friend. Not as in slobbering, wagging your tail, or humping someone's leg. Not as in "fetch" and "good boy." Not in that har-har buddy boy, slap on the back way. But in the confident and direct way that good solid leadership makes everyone's lives better and easier. In this way the Alpha who takes on the responsibility takes responsibility off everyone else. In this way the person who takes the primary risk allows everyone else some breathing room. In this way the troubles and frustrations and challenges of the group become the headache of one man or woman. Although they are not always recognized or appreciated, these are the gifts you as an Alpha give to others in the workplace as "Man's Best Friend." Consider the slobber an extra if you get it.

The Role of a Leader

Being Real with Yourself and Others

Good leaders understand there are roles they must play. Situations and people dictate different approaches. For me, depending on what day it is, I can be a best friend, worst enemy, figurehead, father-confessor, brutal competitor, ass-chewer, parent, strategist, warrior, statesman, salesman, negotiator, diplomat, or asshole-in-charge. This is the chameleon-like nature that a good leader must possess to get the best results. But in some of these leadership roles we are tempted to think, speak, or behave differently or at odds with who we really are. It can become a conjured up "fake you" trying to manipulate people or a situation. You have probably seen it in others you have worked for or with, and it causes loss of respect. This is a compromise I hope to help you avoid. I have been there and back and can say that not being true to yourself is no way to lead or live. Your main role is always to be yourself when it comes to values, integrity, and self-pride. Wow. What a basic concept. Being real. What a challenge. What a burden. Just being who you really are.

You do not want people wondering who you are. You want your team to share the same value system. One person sets the tone and example for values, integrity, and growth. Leading and motivating others is impossible if you are not being yourself. Situational leaders breed situational followers.

Lots of guys think that people will not respect them if they don't put up a hard front, even if it is not who they really are. Lots of guys think that being real is being "soft." That is fear and lack of confidence talking. Being yourself, positively, unapologetically, and straight up, is something people respect. People don't have to try to figure out what your agenda is. They aren't trying to filter out the "fake you" factor. Love you or hate you, you are always better being yourself 24-7. So then, if everyone hates you, disrespects you, or thinks poorly of you, you probably really are an incompetent, unpleasant asshole. But at least you can be sure of it.

Real vs. Fake Alpha

The work world is full of people who want to be strong Alphas but are unwilling to take the long, hard road to becoming one. Instead, they display behaviors they think give them a dominant or controlling position from which they can defend their internal weaknesses. These are fake Alpha leaders.

These people usually do more damage to others and their organizations than good. They are always working against the team concept. They are usually working from a place of cynicism and negativity. They are unable to evolve from a self-centered view of the world. None of these traits serves the mission of an organization.

What is the cure? It is up to that person's superiors and peers to call him out on these irrelevant and overbearing behaviors. Most of the time this does not happen because everyone wants to avoid rocking the boat. Well, guess what—the boat is already rocking and taking on water. It is everyone's job to help stabilize it by getting Mr. Fake Alpha to sit his ass down.

There is a difference between real and fake Alpha behavior and leadership. Here are a few clues when you are sorting things out:

Real Alphas are:

- Confident
- Driven
- Truthful
- Inspired
- Motivated
- Proud
- Goal-oriented

Fake Alphas are:

- Insecure (so they overcompensate)
- Egotistical (so it's not about the work outcomes but about them)
- Externally motivated (they use the world as a mirror that they have to prove something to)

Real Alphas:

- See people as a challenge and resource
- Balance self-interests with those of employees and the organization

Fake Alphas:

- Always see people as competitors or in comparison to themselves
- Sometimes put self before organization and always before employees

When you see someone doing something that is so patently fake-Alpha and stupid in a leadership role, you can be pretty sure the person's responsibility has exceeded his or her ability to handle it—and, worse, the person probably even knows it.

Real Alphas: The Iditarod Winning Formula

In the course of researching this book I traveled to Jackson Hole in Wyoming to visit with Frank Teasley, a world-famous dogsled racer. Frank has also competed in the Iditarod race in Alaska multiple times. I wanted to understand what really makes a dog an "Alpha" under the most competitive and extreme conditions and to see whether there were any lessons in it for our industry.

At Frank's remote location, he and his wife raise 170 sled dogs. From these they select teams that compete in Europe, Alaska, and around the continental U.S. When I got out of the truck, I was greeted with a loud symphony of howls, barks, and cries. It seemed a huge chaotic mix of over-excited animals. What I was actually looking at was an Olympic training ground for some of the most amazing animal athletes in the world.

After a warning not to get too close to some of the dogs (these are not cocker spaniels), I was given the opportunity to drive my own sled team. Six dogs were harnessed to my sled for a twenty-five mile run. The temperature was minus 10 plus wind chill. My Alpha dog, harnessed at the front, was Esky. She was a veteran of the Iditarod and had run thousands of miles under the most difficult of circumstances. I was damn lucky that Esky knew what she was doing because my learning curve was just beginning.

It took the dogs about fifteen minutes to hit their stride. In that same fifteen minutes I stopped feeling my frozen face, hands, and feet. Besides that, it turned out that controlling the team was complex, based on the individual leader and the composition of the team. No matter a raw rookie like me or 1,100 miles across the frozen Alaska wilderness—the qualities of the team started with the very front dog. The mushers were very clear that there are major differences among all 170 dogs. So for research purposes I had to know—how do they select their top dogs? How do they decide between all of these high-performance animals to select the top teams to compete around the world? What characteristics might also apply to our top foremen and superintendents? What lessons could be learned?

The true Alpha dog that gets to the elite racing level has three key characteristics. These are as follows:

- *Desire*

The most important aspect to begin with for these dogs is the ability and burning desire to go hard. When you walk up to the sled, these dogs start howling and crying like you are stealing their souls. They strain in their harnesses and jump into the air, trying to break the sled free. They live to run. They live to work. Nothing gives them greater pleasure and purpose than pulling and running hard. Are humans so different? Can any leader really succeed without the willingness to "go hard"? Leaders have to find pleasure and purpose in hard work. Leaders have to have the stamina to keep pushing themselves and their teams in a way that separates them from the ordinary performer. Alpha leaders may find themselves restless and anxious if they are not pushing hard. Their natural state of intensity is a little bit higher than those around them.

- *Aggressiveness*

The top Alphas are bred for aggressiveness. These dogs are not little cuddly puppies. The exact words used by one musher were: "You want a dog that would fight to the death but won't pick fights with the rest of his team." Though it is not an absolute necessity that an Alpha leader be highly aggressive, it is a typical trait in our industry. It is unlikely that someone who is passive will do well as a construction leader. Aggressiveness is a trait shared by man and beast alike, but clearly there is a profile that balances unyielding fierceness and team cooperation. Again, this combination of aggressiveness and team orientation is something very transferable to leadership in the construction workplace.

- *Intelligence*

Perhaps the most important element for a real Alpha dog is smarts. You can have stamina, desire, and aggressiveness, but without the brains to capitalize on these you have a basic brute mentality. On the sled there were verbal commands that guided the team: "hike" (go), "gee" (right), "haw" (left), "whoa" (obvious), "easy" (slow down together while maintaining tension on harness), and "get up" (push harder while going up hill). A dog racer in competition may be going between 15–18 mph. In case you don't think that sounds very fast, try flying, bumping, and skidding along frozen trails at that rate behind sixteen dogs. Intelligence means they know what to do when given a command—immediately, consistently, and dependably. It also means that the musher/leader cultivates and values intelligence. In construction you often hear stupid phrases being used with apprentices such as, "You're not paid to think." That is the old school "I'm in charge" tradition killing opportunity. Construction today is all about creating knowledge-based workers, not just dumb guys to pull the sled.

So, in summary, what are the Alpha lessons learned? Character is more important than skills. Without desire and stamina, knowledge is nothing. Adversity of conditions filters for top performers. Strong Alpha personalities need to value teamwork. Aggressiveness is necessary but not at the expense of the crew. Intelligence that is well directed and supported is the most important aspect of a high-performance team. Oh, and finally, if you want to make them happy, don't just pet Alphas; give them a job to do.

Understanding Dominance and the Pack

Wolves and wild dogs live and work in packs. They are highly intelligent and social in their interactions. They do everything for a reason and in the interest of the pack. Thus, it seems curious that when two wolves fight for dominance, the pack often surrounds them, waiting for one or the other to be severely injured. It is documented that in many cases when one wolf hurts another badly, the pack will jump in and tear the loser apart. This analogy applies more than you can know in the world of Alpha leaders.

There come times when every leader is tested, by employees, bosses, competitors, clients—you name it. Someone is going to try to test you. I began in a CEO position at age twenty-six. This put a big, fat target on my back. Competitors saw it as their opportunity to kill off our organization. Good old boys wanted to run me off, just to amuse themselves. Tough field guys thought I was just a jerk college boy. The pack had circled. The test was going to determine my fate. I was going to prevail or get torn apart. In these cases, as a strategic method of building both respect and caution on the part of others, you have to assert your capability and dominance. There can be no question of the consequences of taking you on. Especially in a male-dominated industry like construction, there is a lot of testosterone and all the rough interaction that comes with it.

Now, this does not mean pick a fight with everyone who pushes your buttons; it means you have to let people know:

- That you will not be pushed around or intimated
- That your age, gender, race, family ties, or anything not related to your performance and position are irrelevant
- That you see yourself as their leader or peer and will demand respect accordingly
- That there will be serious consequences to pushing you, and that they should learn that cooperation is a better way to approach you

- That if it comes to conflict, you will not shy from it and, if there are stakes involved, you will aggressively advocate your position

So I was tested by the pack. Everyone pushed. Some to take advantage and others just to see what I would do. It represented a few very rough years for me. It caused me more than a few sleepless nights and bad cases of heartburn. It made me ask more than once if I really wanted the responsibility and conflict that came with senior leadership. But since I did want it, I had no alternative. Simply put, I could not take any shit, and I was forced to come on strong in many situations. I knew that if I did not do this successfully early in my leadership role, I would be marginalized and disrespected due to my age and perceived inexperience. My personal branding was on the line. And if I was seen as weak, the court of construction leadership opinion might never allow me to recover. Pushing back was the only way for me to survive and succeed in an industry full of very tough and determined people.

You note I also use the term "survive" above. Does this seem a little melodramatic? Well, let's go back to the pack and why they make that circle and kill off the loser in the fight. When the pack (crew, office, industry competitors, and so on…) circle up to watch two individuals in conflict, it is not to watch for amusement. The way that conflict turns out may indicate to the pack whether the loser still belongs or if his or her weakness is a fatal flaw that must be eliminated. The pack knows that weakness in one reflects weakness in all. Are we so different from the wolves? How quick are we to judge others for their courage or lack thereof? How fast are we to identify those unable to maintain the level of group performance necessary? How often do we tolerate the uncommitted, incompetent, or incapable?

A leader is by default put in a highly visible position. Thus, all the highly aggressive and ambitious pack members can be expected eventually to test or challenge the lead Alpha. It is normal. It is the way of nature. It is the way of business. It is the way the pack thrives and succeeds. Leading well will require conflict and pushing back; just make sure it is about the best interests of the pack as much as it is about you.

Avoiding Positional Leadership

Avoid "positional" leadership. Positional leadership is a one-dimensional way to lead by simply combining your job title and power. The fact that someone has a position of authority often makes it easy to get his or her way. It is the position in charge, not the person. The use of the leverage and power of the position speeds up the process of decision making but often at a hidden cost. Positional leadership also reduces the potential to obtain buy-in. It can inhibit or eliminate point-counterpoint analysis. The necessary "devil's advocate" role within your team will not be voiced or examined. At worst it can also reflect things like "We've always done it that way." Positional leadership does not allow any form of constructive input or dissent. Do not rely on your title or position to convince others to follow you. Win them over by showing respect, and your title will be seen as earned in full.

Maintaining Consistency in Leadership

Leadership consistency in manner, practice, and action is very important. The quality and intensity of your Alpha effort needs to be matched by consistency. It does not matter what your style is; it matters that people can depend upon it. You can't have super-high highs and low lows. You have to be steady at the wheel. This is difficult. We all have off days. We all have ups and downs. But if you bring these things to work as a leader, you are going to make your team anxious. People are going to wonder and lose confidence in you. Consistency is the safe zone you bring as a platform for their best efforts. They want to know that they are not going to get surprised by you going off on a tangent. Consistency breeds confidence. Consistency makes you dependable. Consistency breeds trust.

Leadership and Fear of Failure

Most people have some personal fear of failure, which can be either a motivating force in life or a barrier to advancement. But fear of failure is very personal. It needs a personal strategy. Courage is really the only solution.

When people struggle with fear of failure, they often cannot see the strengths and tools at their disposal. Fear of failure tends to magnify only those things we see as negative about ourselves. Leaders who cannot see themselves accurately may succumb to fear or failure. If they cannot see themselves in the best light, then they cannot really see their subordinates with the same clarity. In the construction workplace fear of failure can:

- Push people toward blaming others for problems instead of solving them
- Create overcompensation with ego or bluster when leaders are uncertain about dealing with people or situations
- Erode confidence in leadership ability and continuous growth
- Detract from the ability to develop subordinates as they become a perceived threat
- Lead to meeting constructive criticism with defensiveness rather than treating it as a learning experience

It is very important to assess the impact of fear of failure on how you, your peers, and subordinates perform. A great organization or team works to eliminate this barrier through advanced training and tools to build courage and self-confidence. The organization must also treat failure as a learning event, not a blame event. It is safe to say that we only achieve what we see ourselves capable of. Tapping courage and leveraging it personally and professionally can make a real organizational difference as a long-term strategy.

Risk, Fear, and Leadership

Beyond personal fear of failure, overall risk tolerance is important for anyone interested in leadership advancement. There are many levels of risk tolerance stratified throughout our society. But it is rare outside of highly bureaucratic organizations (think government or other public sector jobs) that anyone with low risk tolerance advances to significant levels of responsibility. Leadership requires a high tolerance for risk. Risk is about fear. Managing this risk and overcoming this fear is a leadership requirement.

My personal risk tolerance is very high. I have skydived, run with the bulls in Pamplona, rafted class V rivers, climbed 14,000 foot mountains, and trekked the Amazon jungle and Sahara desert. Scarier than any of that was speaking solo to an audience of four thousand people. I was so nervous that I could not control my heart rate, and my vision actually got blurry right before I went on stage. Petrified as I was, I managed it. I can't say I enjoyed it at that moment, but the feeling afterward was worth the serious discomfort. I guess I consider fear a performance-improvement tool.

For me the pursuit of risk and overcoming fear bring clarity. They focus my talent and test my abilities. There is no excuse in the moment for my action or inaction. I look at this as a hardcore method of mental training. If you can train your mind to overcome fear and accept risk, then even stuff you never thought you could handle can become fairly routine.

This is the path you travel as you rise up in leadership position and responsibility. As you rise up, the risks, responsibilities, and consequences seem to get bigger (and scarier). You have to become more and more comfortable taking the risks associated with independent decision making: people and resource management, strategic and logistical planning, problem solving, and execution. Is it stressful? It can be. Is it a pain in the ass sometimes? Absolutely. Is it a rush and a feeling unlike anything else? Yes. Risk and fear can be the greatest motivators and intoxicants you can find. They can also be deer-in-the-headlights paralyzing. Finding out your limits and then stretching them is a personal and professional journey that has some incredible payoffs. Risk and fear are part of the normal price of embracing leadership responsibilities. Lean into it; it is worth it. Trust me.

The Price of Arrogance

If I had a dollar for every time I was an arrogant leader (in my twenties and early thirties), I could have bought a Ferrari. Yes, this ridiculous behavior is common in leaders—and most often a by-product of insecurity or insensitivity. Mine was. How about one out of a hundred stories I could tell?

So I was at a major event with all my key contractors. In my hurry to catch up to a few of them upon arrival, I took my truck keys and tossed them at my number two right-hand person. I said, "Hey, move my truck" and took off. About three minutes later I turned around and she was standing there. She threw the keys back at me and said, "Move it yourself." Now, in replaying the moment, I see what an arrogant asshole I really was. No "Hi." No "Please." No taking a moment. No sensitivity. No emergency requiring such action. I was treating her worse than I would a valet at a restaurant. She wasn't going to take my shit—and bravo for her. Of course, when she threw the keys at me, I started to get mad, but quickly I did move my own truck and apologized to her for my lack of manners and respect. The problem is that it took me another hundred episodes (in which people did not confront me) to start to address the problem. Arrogant assholeitis.

The most arrogant are often the most insecure. Their arrogance is a veneer covering up the fear that others might judge them. And arrogant leaders generally do not assign any price for their indulgence. Well, here are the top five "costs of being arrogant":

1. Arrogant leaders generally alienate their followers.
2. Arrogant leaders are rarely worth mentoring up to the next level as they are not interested in self-improvement or able to ask for help.
3. Arrogant leaders are usually terrible listeners; thus, they miss major opportunities.
4. Arrogant leaders usually put their image before strategy.
5. Arrogant leaders rarely admit mistakes; thus, they model poor behavior for peers and subordinates.

How much growth or profit is left on the table due to overly arrogant leadership? Only you know within your organization.

The Five Temptations of Power

Power is a weird thing. It is hard to describe it exactly at a personal level, but it is very visible when it is being used. Do not succumb to these five temptations when you are using power:

1. Using it to make yourself feel important at the expense of others or the organization
2. Using it to benefit yourself before others or the organization
3. Compromising your integrity, values, or ethics because you can
4. Giving less effort because you are in charge and accountable to no one
5. Mistaking power for competence or talent

(Watch for) The Seduction of Success

Although many leaders are more worried about failure, what they really should be worried about is success. Success seduces. Success whispers in your ear. Success more than anything allows you to rationalize whatever you do. If you can point to profit dollars, positive outcomes, or a good job title, then you have a strong excuse to do whatever you want. Success can become an excuse. Success can kill your work ethic. Success can make you lay back. Success can bring about boredom. Success can sometimes stand as an obstacle to constant improvement and to monitoring and evaluating performance or systems.

The old saying, "If it ain't broke, don't fix it" came from somewhere, and you can bet the guy who said it was a wise man, a wise man who was into the status quo. Ask yourself right now if you have ever used past success as a rationale for current action or inaction. Don't be ashamed. I would be surprised if you hadn't worked success to your advantage. The funny part is that most everyone who is successful has done it—which truly is the lamest excuse of all.

Be a Magnetic and Positive Leader

A magnetic and positive person draws positive people and outcomes to themselves. This ability is vital to success at work. If you do not work at being positive, you may, without even knowing it, put out negative energy and draw negativity to yourself. Now, before you think I'm dropping some California tofu-eater metaphysical B.S. on you, give me a chance.

Being positive is very important. Being respected is, to my way of thinking, always better than being liked—but what if you can achieve both? What are some of the business benefits? Positive and magnetic people:

- Are better persuaders and negotiators
- Are given the benefit of the doubt about their intentions
- Generally have more doors open to them
- Often have a network of people promoting them
- Attract others
- Make people smile

Okay, that last one is a "have a nice day" (barf) moment. But it is real.

A lot of people think that being positive is simply inherent—either people are positive or not. And so they are sometimes unwilling to work at it. I disagree. Being positive is a choice. Here's what to keep in mind if you want to be positive and magnetic both in and out of the workplace:

- Be enthusiastic and show it.
- Be encouraging and say it.
- Be complimentary and mean it.
- Show real interest in other people and their families.
- Be a good and active listener.
- Don't interrupt others.
- Show respect and make people feel important.
- And remember, as Dale Carnegie said wisely, "A person's name is the sweetest and most important sound they can ever hear…."

Some leaders and managers revel in the idea that being a hard ass whom people fear or dislike is a good sign. Personally, I think being a positive and encouraging hard ass is a much better idea.

Leadership, Integrity, and the Death of the Handshake

I have heard for many years the lament over the loss of integrity and "the handshake" that once defined the construction industry. It was an unspoken honor system that governed relations and business more than any contract ever could. Where did the handshake go? It was not just one great dark cloud that swept away the handshake but small chips knocked out from the foundations of trust and ethics in business. Now, many years and chips later, the costs have become highly visible, as has a general acceptance of "situational ethics" as a price that must be paid if one is to avoid being "rolled." Must it be this way? Not entirely.

There may be many who think the phrase "ethical construction" is an oxymoron. And in the very complex, competitive, and unforgiving world of our industry, it often is. Survival in the business now demands that one look over his or her shoulder at all times because the naïve and trusting pay the price more often than the hardened cynics do.

I have seen it all, as have you: delayed or denied payments, ugly claims, unacknowledged bad specs, brutal subcontracts, skimpy bid protests, back-door clauses, agency false claim threats, bogus employee lawsuits or workers comp claims, change orders uncompensated, lying, shakedown lawsuits, bid shopping, embezzlement, employee mistreatment, time card padding, theft of materials, general CYA, and worse. So what to do in a Darwinian environment that does not provide a direct incentive for ethical behavior and business practice? Everybody bends. Everybody rationalizes. Everybody lives in the gray area. This is not just in our industry. Multiple surveys also indicate that more than eighty percent of high school students admit to cheating, and it's not much better in college. Integrity is becoming an option in our society. Now, I'm not foolish enough to call for perfection or to sit in judgment of others. I'm simply observing an area of business in need of improvement, with a significant potential for economic reward.

Organizational leadership requires alignment with some form of values that you, your managers, employees, and clients clearly understand. So the first question is: What are the values (visible and invisible) at work in your organization? And are ethical practices a part of these values? According to the Conference Board, a national business leadership organization, some seventy-five percent or more of companies have a code of ethics as a part of their business plans and operations. The question is why (besides simply to look good)?

Let's take a quick look at some of the building blocks of ethical behavior:

- Wisdom and knowledge
- Self-control and discipline
- Value of others vs. self
- Courage and integrity

What business leader would not want an organization populated by individuals who possess these characteristics? Is it a stretch to think that having an organization built on these values might have some competitive advantages?

The primary business benefits are trust and loyalty. Putting a price tag on these is pretty difficult, especially if you stand to lose an opportunity now and then as a result. But truth, trust, and loyalty are foundational elements. A lack of them will destroy a business's image, relationships and brand. This is a lesson that can come too late; when no one wants to do business with you, it is past time to take a hard look at your ethics in policy and practice.

Your leadership ethic is most important of all. If leaders cannot display uncompromising integrity and ethics, they simply invite less than that among their employees and associates. Every year at my company every employee goes through a 360 Review. Every employee anonymously rates everyone else on sixteen key attributes we have decided define our organizational values. I am rated along with everyone else on issues such as trustworthiness, office politics, and integrity. I don't always get top marks on every category, but every year I publicly post the results of my 360 Review on my door for everyone to see. Sometimes this is no fun for me. But a leader is being watched every minute, and every action is a signal of what is acceptable or encouraged. No organization can, in my opinion, create business success and fulfilled, motivated employees with internal ethical disconnect. Crappy ethics in a company leads to all kinds of conflict, politics, and financial impacts. Look at the leader, and most often you'll find the source of it.

There are proactive steps you can take within your company or even the industry. Some basics you should consider might include the following:

1. Identify the values and principles by which you want your organization and your people to be known.

2. Adopt or develop an ethics policy for your organization or agency that directly supports these values and communicate it down to the last guy in the field.

3. Reward and highlight ethical practices by staff.

4. Outline consequences for unethical practices and do not compromise.

5. Promote your ethical values, principles, and policies as part of your organizational brand, culture, and identity to your clients.

Though the handshake may be close to dead, it does not mean that honor and integrity are not still a choice. It's an individual choice, best influenced by leaders, businesses, and an industry that values it. Like you.

Professional Decision Maker

What Do You Need to Know to Make a Decision?

I read an article on effective leadership and management claiming that most of the time the average leader has to make decisions with less than seventy percent of the information necessary available to him or her. What does this mean?

- That if you insist on waiting for 100 percent of the information, you may stall organizational momentum

- That leaders have to be very intuitive about how much information is enough

- That leaders usually cannot go back and blame lack of information for bad decisions as they are in charge of balancing quantity of data with good judgment

- That something has to fill in the information percentage gap
- That having to have every single detail covered before you make a decision is not usually a great leadership behavior
- That time rarely permits us to spend excessive time examining and analyzing
- That due to time constraints many decisions must be made without total and complete data

These are not excuses for hasty or sloppy management or superficial treatment of key issues. But they do challenge top leaders to be very judicious when looking at the time vs. detail decision continuum.

If you have to make decisions without all the data, then you want to pay attention to limiting your downside risks. Here are some key strategies to moderate downside risk:

- Ask yourself, "What if it all goes wrong?" What is the absolutely worst consequence? If you can live with that, go forward.
- Do you have a contingency plan you could engage in if your decision goes bad? Or have you burned all your bridges behind you?
- Know what approach will be taken when you get conflicting advice or data. Don't be swayed by anyone's reaction to not taking his or her recommended course of action.

Decide and Act. Period.

Once you have made a decision, don't re-analyze it until it plays out. Sometimes it is very tempting to immediately start re-analyzing the decision you have made. This often leads to doubt, anxiety, and more questions. It is hard to focus on putting your decision into action if you are still questioning yourself. Further, as a leader, others will perceive your uncertainty. If you are making a commitment to a particular action, let it play out. Also, don't shy away from your decision at the first sign of prospective failure or complication. Nine out of ten problems you see coming down the road at your course of action will veer off into the ditch on their own. Decide and act. Then leave it alone.

Avoiding Second-Guessing

You've heard the term "second-guessing" before I'm sure. I've never really understood what it meant. Where was the "first guess"? What people mean is revisiting a decision or action and going through all the coulda-woulda-shouldas.

When you are the responsible party for making decisions, you have to be willing to stand by them in the face of challenges from others even after the fact. These could come from either your superiors or your subordinates. I can tell you that in twenty-five years of leadership many people have second-guessed some of my most important decisions. I have been under some pretty serious pressure to change my decisions in the face of overwhelming doubt and criticism.

Others second-guessing me started to make me second-guess myself. But this is what differentiates effective and bold leaders from simple managers—those who willingly take the "second-guessing" heat that comes with decision making versus those who test the political winds before pressing ahead or change their convictions under duress.

Do not succumb to second-guessing, peer pressure, or over-analysis. No one I have ever known makes better decisions the second time before the first one has played through.

Using Logic vs. Your Gut

When making decisions, a good leader has to balance logic against instinct. Too much dependence on just one or the other is not a good thing, so let's look at both as tools for your use. Let's begin with instinct or "your gut."

You have certainly heard about the importance of "first impressions." This advice doesn't just concern trying to create a favorable opinion of yourself; it's also about influencing instinctual and intuitive decision making. Why is it that you get a "vibe" from people and situations? How is it that you can within minutes and even sometimes seconds decide how you are going to interact with certain people? Such responses reveal your instinct or intuition in operation. What follows is based only on my opinion and experience, but I would strongly suggest that you listen very closely.

Some of the worst business and personal decisions I have ever made were the product of not having listened to my instincts. I let so-called facts and data get in the way. I brushed aside instinctive red flags due to time constraints or a perceived opportunity. Almost without exception, my instincts told me one thing, yet still I did another.

You don't have to depend completely on your gut, which can be just as big a problem. If you go with your instincts and don't do enough homework, then you are gambling and trying to go off of your track record. Gamblers who don't understand the game they are playing and the cards on the table soon lose everything. People who are impatient will often go with their guts because data and logic bore them. People who don't like to plan or who are unorganized will also try to use instinct as a substitute for a logically constructed game plan. These are key elements to watch for in yourself and those who work for you.

Finally, try to balance logic and instinct with all your decisions, but if it is a struggle, my advice is to trust your instincts.

What Is Urgent vs. Important?

Making decisions about controlling your time and utilizing your talent requires you to be thoughtful and strategic. Without these attributes you may spend almost every day at work placing urgent matters first. What does that look like? Have you ever had a day when you feel you worked your ass off and got nothing done? That's a day of selecting urgent issues instead of important ones.

Do not mistake urgency for importance. Do not think that because a fire is burning it warrants your immediate attention every time. A lot of the time those fires burn themselves out. Do not think that jumping from one thing to another to another is good leadership. You have to learn the difference between what is urgent and important.

If you look at the box above, you can easily see how to categorize any of the things that need your attention. Everything you do fits into one of the boxes from one to four. Let's take a look at what might fit into these boxes for purposes of analysis:

Box 1: Urgent and Important (Take Action Now)

These are things that need attention now. Both the critical nature of the issue and immediate timing combine in this box. Some examples would be:

- Responses to key clients
- Decisions where time or money is on the line
- Deadline-driven projects, tasks, or important commitments
- Critical decisions that cannot be made by subordinates

Box 2: Urgent But Not Important (Don't Be Reactive)

These are things that are time-driven and may or may not be worthy of your action. Because of habit or others' needs we can sometimes get lost in urgent but not important activities, which become matters of "daily firefighting." A lot of work is involved but not much really gets done. Seems urgent but not important items include:

- 50 percent of all phone calls
- 80 percent of all email
- 95 percent of text messages
- Problems brought to you by others for you to solve that they have not tried to solve themselves
- Personnel issues that can and should wait
- Any form of employee venting, frustration, or emotional dumping that does not lead to resolutions

Box 3: Important But Not Urgent (Be Proactive)

There are things that are important but that don't jump out as vital sometimes. Time spent on these things, though, directly improves the bottom line results of the organization. It is at your peril that you ignore these things. Examples of important but not urgent would include:

- Planning
- Evaluating people

- Evaluating systems
- Client relationship building

Box 4: Not Important and Not Urgent (Be Disciplined and Ignore)

We live in a multitasking world where immediate reaction is standard behavior. Especially young people today think they need to respond moment to moment with their technology. This is indulgent and simply a bad habit to be addressed. This is a key area where major chunks of time are wasted.

Not urgent and not important is the way a lot of poor planners fill their time. It's the stuff people do when they are reactive instead of proactive. It often involves people who have excessive social needs at work. It means inaction. This is bad stuff.

Get your boxes lined up. Make sure you pay very close attention to boxes 1 and 3. These are what good leaders attend to most of the time.

A Pro Leaves Time to Think

In a high-pressure, high-production environment many leaders spend the vast majority of time "doing" tasks. If someone came into your office or onto the jobsite and you were just sitting there, apparently doing nothing, how weird would that be? It might be that you just sitting there thinking could be of the greatest benefit to your organization. But could you do it guilt-free?

There is a story about Henry Ford (a ball-busting tyrant of a business leader if there ever was one) and how he hired an efficiency expert to go through his entire operation as well as his factories.

The expert provided a very bad report to Ford about one of his managers, whom he had seen several times just sitting there with his feet up, apparently doing nothing. Ford responded, "That man had an idea several years ago that saved this company millions of dollars. I believe he had his feet in the same position at the time. You just leave him alone."

Real breakthroughs in process and with people don't always come as a result of task-driven approaches. They come from allowing yourself the time and flexibility to think. Planning is thinking. Evaluating is thinking. Strategizing is thinking. All of these have great value to leaders. If you are limited to "doing," it is likely that is all you will ever "do."

One of my construction mentors once told me that he just lies in bed for almost an hour in the morning after waking up. He's thinking about the day's plan. I kind of thought that was weird and a waste of time until I remembered he has built a huge company starting with only an apprenticeship and a pickup truck. While his five hundred employees are getting ready to start "doing," he is lying there "thinking." The lesson is that the power of one guy thinking puts five hundred more guys to work.

Thinking always comes before doing. So if no one is taking the time to think (including you), then how are you ever going to do things better or different? My tip: Do some of your planning and thinking the night before. Be clear in your thought processes about what you want to accomplish. Make your notes or lists. Let the night be a time for your mind to work on it, and greet the day in execution mode. Also, don't ever feel like stopping to think is a waste of time. More money and time have been lost for lack of this simple approach in the construction industry than for perhaps any other single reason.

Acknowledge and Use Your Bad Decisions

As previously noted, I have made some really bad decisions. I have totally failed, and there is no way to put a happy face on it. So afterward I have faced three choices. I could pretend it didn't happen (and try to cover myself). I could become defensive and rationalize my decision (and tell anyone who will listen what I was thinking and why I decided it that way). Or I could use the situation as a case study and tell people not to screw up the way I did. As painful as it is, I have most always chosen the third option.

Most every person who has worked for me has heard my epic failure stories. My poor management. My bad hires. My terrible presentations and blown relationships. My mistakes in strategy. Usually, these come up as part of helping, reconstructing, or chewing employees' asses off about their own serious mistakes. No leader is on such a pedestal that he or she does not err in judgment or strategy. But more importantly, you don't want people to start taking less risk or accepting less responsibility as a result of bad decisions or outcomes. You will remember most of your really bad decisions anyway, so why not put them to work for you?

Use Courage and Confidence While Making Mistakes

So we have clearly established that I have been stupid many times and deserve a big "L" for loser on my forehead for my leadership blunders. But at the same time, I am among the best at what I do in North America. How can both these statements be true?

You are going to mess up in the public eye. In front of your team, your clients, your boss…count on it; you are going to step in it. And I want you to hold your head high, put on your best face, and maintain confidence while you are scraping it off your shoes. Overreaction to mistakes and errors can be the downfall of many good leaders. They shave off self-confidence. They erode our desire to take risk. They replace ambition with caution. Let me tell you a little story about messing up big time.

I was speaking to a few hundred top national leaders on business strategy and development. I was using a joke to illustrate a point, and I had everyone on the edge of their seats as I forgot the punch line. I said, "So he bet the hundred dollars, and the dog goes over the hill and then…and then…" And then what? And then I forgot the damn punch line.

I mean my brain just died. Blank screen. No input. Like someone vacuumed out my head. I looked up to see hundreds of people staring at me, waiting. I tried again to finish the joke, and I started to kind of mumble and garble. My heart rate went straight up to 220. My hands got sweaty immediately. My hair was standing up straight and on fire. And I knew there was only one way out. Acknowledge total failure. Find courage and confidence in the midst of disaster.

So I told them: "Guys, I forgot the punch line."

They just looked at me like what kind of idiot is this guy? He is supposed to be a national industry expert, and he can't even remember his own jokes? That was a moment in which my head had to stay high. That was a moment when I could not fold up under pressure. So I went on. And calmed down. And delivered the rest of the program.

So as we got to the very end of the day, I was finishing the program. I ended the entire program and concluded with this: "And the last thing for the day is…so the dog goes over the hill…," and I finished the joke and hammered home the punch line. And they loved it. They thought I did it on purpose.

Self-confidence and courage are all you will have to lean on sometimes. When you fail and have nothing left, admit the error with honesty and class. Don't let it show too much, and don't replay it a hundred times later. But I will admit I don't tell jokes in professional presentations to big crowds anymore.

"Hey, did you hear the one about the loser guy named Breslin?"

Nothing Fazes the Professional

Due to my bloodlines my emotional eruptions from years back were legendary. My staff always kind of looked forward to them in a weird way. Like a red-line Monster Truck crash. So a couple of years ago they decided to play a mean joke on me. They wrote up a very official document that basically indicated a major company was trying to totally screw us over at the very last minute on a very big deal. They put it on my desk and huddled outside my office, waiting for the volcano to blow. I quietly read it, looked up, and told my assistant, "Call our lawyers. Send them the brief. And take a look at contract section C again for our strongest arguments." And then I turned away and started working on something else. My staff was floored. What they had expected to be a big joke on me became a lesson for them. I showed them that my emotions were secondary to getting the job done. I also modeled the mature response for dealing with things that cannot be changed or modified at that moment. They got the message; nothing fazes the professional.

This is not to say you always have to be cool and detached. Do I still get pissed off? Yes. Do I still get "excitable" at times? Yes. Does someone come close my office door when F-bombs fly? I admit it still does happen. Sometimes it is strategic, and other times it is just the worst part of my nature coming out. In any event, the key here is to try not to allow yourself to be riled or ruled by reactions. Don't let them interfere with your decision making. Don't show your employees that emotions are the way to deal with each other or project difficulties. Yelling, cursing, complaining, venting, or whining on any ongoing basis diminishes anyone as a person and leader. Nothing fazes the professional.

Understanding the Business You Are In

The difference between being a high-performance construction leader and just another foreman or lead-man is understanding the big picture. You must see how your decisions can impact the big picture. What is the big picture? Let's define it as the world beyond your immediate responsibilities, priorities, and jobsite. Information not essential to your actions today provides the advanced knowledge you are going to need tomorrow. It is about really understanding the "business that you are in."

Some will say I already understand the business I'm in. I raise iron or build roads or lay pipes or set turbines or weld or paint or…. These are the wrong answers. These are the tasks that people do at work. That is only a general description of the work, not the business. Let me be more specific on questions that can provide you with the big picture:

- Could you name your organization's top ten clients?
- Do you know the ratio of jobs that are bid to those you obtain?
- Do you know who the main players are in your industry and what makes them competitive and relevant and different from one another?
- Could you identify one major change that will occur in your business in the next three years? What could or should be done to meet it?
- Can you tell me how technology is changing and will change your job and the future of your industry segment?
- Can you identify the approximate net profit margin of your industry?
- Do you know what are the main variables and drivers of that margin?
- Could you explain how bonding, finances, or lines of credit impact your company or organization?
- Do you know about project delivery alternatives and why they are critical to the future of the construction industry?
- Could you tell me five common questions that arise for a company seeking to pre-qualify for select bidders' lists and how they relate to your job now?
- What industry trade journals or websites are most important to your industry, and how many do you read each month?

If you know the answers to these questions, then you have the big picture, and I congratulate you. I struggle to keep up with the business even after twenty-five years on the frontline. I have to read almost half an hour a day. I have to ask people older and younger than I what they think is really going on. I have to keep up with technology that seems to be leaving me behind. The questions above represent only a few examples of what it takes to be a growing professional in the industry. Professionals need a broader view of the industry than the project they are on, the bid they are putting through, or the fire they are putting out. Assuming bigger responsibility means understanding the bigger picture. Get interested in the big picture, and others in positions of authority will become more interested in you.

Understanding Client Relations and Satisfaction

The construction industry does not build things. The construction industry satisfies customers and clients who pay to have things built.

Who pays for everyone and everything in the construction industry? It is always the client. This fact is often poorly communicated down the ranks in construction and seems completely lost at the site of construction. It is very important that all your employees understand that a satisfied client is paramount to a successful project. A company's or organization's reputation, brand, and identity are all formed by client satisfaction. Employees must understand this truth and grasp their role. They must connect their efforts on the job to client satisfaction as well as their company's reputation. They must see how their economic relationship with the client is personal.

Many construction workers do not even understand the concept of serving the client. They think it's about getting the work done. It is a good leader who connects the dots for his team. Here are things the client is going to be most concerned about:

- Productivity: is he getting the bang for his construction dollar?
- Safety: is the project being performed safely all the time?
- Quality: is he paying for and getting top quality?

- Schedule: will he get beneficial use of his project on time (or early)?
- Budget: is the project on budget without any price surprises?
- Cooperation: are all the contractors, trades, and employees working cooperatively to meet the client's needs and expectations?
- Credibility: is this organization proving it deserves the next project or opportunity?

Personal Leadership Strategies (PLS) and Tactics

PLS #1: Be the Aborigine: Now Is the Only Time

In the Aborigine culture there is no word for tomorrow. There is also no word for yesterday.

An Aborigine lives now. What is important is happening right this moment. There are no doubts based on yesterday. There is no yesterday. There is no projecting forward into what-ifs. Their full concentration is on what lies before them. They have honed this technique based on the necessity of survival in an incredibly harsh environment. The lesson from the Aborigine is that you need to focus on what is real and now. Can we learn from the past? Absolutely—and we need to take account of it when necessary. Should we attempt to project the future? For sure—planning helps deliver great outcomes. But only if it is strategic and appropriate.

Unlike the Aborigine, most of us spend too much time thinking about the past and future. We do this professionally and personally. We revisit things we cannot ever change. We worry about a future that has not yet arrived. Being immediately present in the now is a very important skill for a good leader. It combines concentration with listening, analysis with instinct, focus with planned action. None of these things is served if you are constantly bouncing between old news and future worries.

For the Aborigine it is simple. If he distracts himself with yesterday or tomorrow, he dies. And thus his language does not serve these concepts, for they are useless in his ongoing quest for success and survival. Be the Aborigine. Not blindly, but deliberately.

PLS #2: Act As If

These three words got me through my first year as a rookie leader. I was not ready to be an Alpha. I was immature. I was one step removed from beer and girls as my top priorities of life. I had no real vision. No life or business experience to lean on. Nothing but sheer will and determination. I figured I was either a leadership experiment or a mistake. Thinking back on it, I was probably both.

Everyone was watching me. Most were just waiting for me to fail. My competition in the industry decided to take me on immediately. My peers resented my rapid advancement. My employees knew I was a raw rookie and suffered for it. What to do while my stomach hurt and I stared at the ceiling many nights at 3 A.M.? Act as if.

This one thing that my predecessor told me helped me get through. Act as if. What does this mean? Not much until it is applied as follows:

- Act as if you have been in the job for years.
- Act as if you have a total grasp of the technical and management aspects of the job.
- Act as if the outcomes you want are going to occur.
- Act as if you are leading the most progressive and successful enterprise in the history of mankind.
- Act as if you have the respect and authority from your employees that should be accorded to the position.
- Act as if the pressure and challenge of the position are things you enjoy (even though they are currently eating away your stomach lining).

The concept is not to fake your way through but to use the power of belief and intent to carry you into the future. In the meantime, if you don't know what you are doing, find a mentor or guide. Admit failure to superiors and get together a game plan to resolve the situation. Don't think that "acting as if" gives you some long-term coverage, because it doesn't. It just fills the gap as you acquire all the necessary knowledge, relationships, tools, and confidence that go with the real thing.

Also remember the phrase is based on the word "act." It does not mean "act" like fake. It means "act" as in perform the role you are in to the highest degree possible until you actually own it. And know that as others watch you they will grow in confidence and trust in you as well.

PLS #3: Know When It's Time

Being a leader means being a negotiator. You will need this skill quite often. There are many complete books on negotiations that are authored by those much more skilled than I am. But in over twenty years of negotiating, I can clearly remember the most important lesson I ever learned from a master mentor.

In the middle of a long and difficult negotiation I was getting more and more frustrated and agitated. There was a lot of pressure, and we were getting nowhere. I was teamed with an older, more experienced guy, and he was just sitting there calm and collected while I was getting more and more impatient and frustrated. I started to get pissed off at him. Finally, I said, "What the hell is wrong with you, man; aren't you going to say something?"

And he simply leaned over, put his hand on my shoulder, and said, "Mark, it isn't time yet."

It took me a while to figure out what he meant, but the master negotiating lesson finally sank in. In every negotiation or complex people situation, you have to be aware of the time it is going to take for all parties to come around. You can't put your personal time clock on the expected outcome. You can't get caught up in the emotional tide of the moment because the shrewd players are watching and waiting until they see that "the time has come" to make the deal, resolve the conflict, press the point, challenge the policy, introduce the initiative…or whatever. Impatient people are often bad negotiators. The person who wants or needs the deal because of time usually does not get the best terms. Timing is a critical part of understanding how to get things done, and remembering that the business clock does not revolve around you is a very valuable negotiating lesson.

PLS #4: Follow the Rules for Rookies

1. Do not mistake your promotion, title, new truck, pat on the back, college degree, or personal confidence for any real competence or ability.

2. Don't give up. As a young or new leader, more people than not will doubt you. It's normal. Simply put, don't back down from your conviction that you can do it, from the confidence necessary to carry out the roles and responsibility, or from challenges or negativity. This does not mean be combative or belligerent or defensive. It just means that you have to expect some rough roads (as noted in other places in this book), so don't give up or back down.

3. Find a mentor. Look a generation ahead for a mentor. This is my most important advice. Look for a man or woman who wants a protégé (or project). What is the mentor getting out of it? The satisfaction of passing on his or her knowledge and expertise. A feeling of being needed. A feeling of importance. A nostalgic reflection of who he or she was at your age. A good mentor will be someone who will model the values, work ethic, and leadership respect you believe will serve you. Do not miss this remarkable opportunity.

PLS #5: Remember: Alpha Is Not Only a Man's World

If you haven't gotten the news, I'd like you to know that Alpha Dog leadership is not just for men. Construction still perpetuates a lot of sexist stereotyping. It tends to have some old-school thinking. It does not always treat women based on talent before gender. Now, before some of you get too puffed up defending your traditional-guy viewpoint, let's revisit our little lessons on nature, dominance, and assertive behavior.

You will note that the most dangerous animals of all are females that are protecting their young. You will note that the hunting and killing in nearly all species is done by the females. We are not even going to talk about black widows or even more Alpha, the female Praying Mantis (bites the head off her mate when she's done with him in the sack). Let me suggest that no one should ever underestimate, pre-judge, or write off the prospective leader status of a woman in the construction world. Talent development and advancement need to be gender-neutral. Some guys think they can still be good old boys or Neanderthals, but in today's world such behavior may just come back to bite them.

PLS #6: Embrace Key Strategies for Women

It is unfortunate that women are sometimes not automatically perceived at the exact peer level as men in the construction workplace. I think women are sometimes judged by a different set of rules. I think that gender can be a barrier for women's advancement. I think that there still exist good-old-boy networks and "boys will be boys" attitudes that do not serve women in leadership very well. I think women generally have a tougher time managing and leading in construction than men. Times are changing, but until they do so more completely, I would like to dedicate the following material to the success and advancement of women in the industry:

1. We all need to recognize and leverage the unique attributes women bring to leadership. I have promoted more women than men to positions of leadership. This is an unusual thing in a field such as construction and engineering, so dominated by strong male personalities. But experience has made me value the positive elements they brought to jobs by comparison with their male counterparts. Women generally:

   - Have less ego driving their decisions
   - Display more concern for the team
   - Have greater attention to schedules, details, and follow-up
   - Serve as better collaborative thinkers and problem solvers
   - Show greater patience
   - Are more motivated by service to others rather than self
   - Derive satisfaction based on pride in completion or accomplishment of a task
   - Can be more likely to share credit and give thanks or appreciation

   All these attributes pay powerful dividends in terms of workplace performance.

2. Women need to be confident in their strengths and abilities. Confidence both real and projected is a key leadership characteristic, especially in construction. Men have a tendency to exhibit confidence whether they really have it or not. Women might tend to underplay theirs as they are generally not as ego-driven. Women have to be comfortable with their key strengths and project belief and confidence in word and action.

3. Women should not have to be like a guy to succeed. Some women, especially those in male-dominated fields, are surrounded by a "guy culture." There is nothing wrong with that, but it should not require them to change their identities and especially not to overcompensate. Women as leaders and managers have their

own competencies that do not require adoption of a rough or masculine manner of communication or style. I have met some very tough, highly skilled women leaders who exude femininity but clearly are going to command respect without compromise. Yes, a woman should have a firm handshake and a notable presence but not at the expense of her true identity.

4. Women may need to push harder for advancement opportunities. In a male-dominated business world those who rise usually do a good job of communicating their ambition and desire to advance. Women sometimes let the quality of their work, diligence, and follow-through speak for them. But in a competitive environment it is very important to push for your own opportunities. The glass ceiling in the office or on the jobsite only gets pushed up from below.

5. Women should look for or set examples. I believe many women aspire to lead and manage but don't always have the role models or mentors to show them the way. Assertively seek them out.

PLS #7: Avoid Napalm on the Campfire (Stress 360)

Are you stressed? Of course you are. We all are. I'm sure there's someone out there who's chilling or chanting or wearing Birkenstocks, working a twenty-hour week, and is stress-free, but I sure as hell don't know them.

No, most people in this business are stressed out one way or another. But that is not a bad thing because we are built that way. A million years ago we had to be prepared to duke it out with a saber-tooth tiger or chase down a wooly mammoth with some of the boys to get some dinner. We are hard-wired to use stress and pressure to perform at a high level as are most other animals.

The problem with us is that we sometimes overdose on stress and pressure. We get ourselves so wound up that our health, relationships, and behaviors are all affected. I know a lot of successful people who are running themselves down and wrecking their health. This is a function of their personal choices. Most stress can be tracked back to our own choices. Not too many people want to hear that, but if they are honest with themselves, they will find that they planted the seeds of their own stress and discomfort.

How does this relate to leadership? Well, simply put, it is hard to be an effective leader if you are on "stress-overdose." One very common characteristic of good Alpha leaders and managers is that they have high thresholds for stress and pressure. Unfortunately, many "Type-A" personalities end up in leadership roles. Adding stress to their already jacked-up personalities can be like dumping napalm on a campfire. Big-time Alphas are also not great about recognizing their limits or asking for help. What we are talking about here is an action-reaction problem that I call Stress 360.

If you are at the point of Stress 360, it is probably showing up in every area of your life. Here are the tests to see whether you are at or approaching Stress 360:

- Sleeping poorly
- Short-tempered at work, home, or both
- Easily distracted
- Difficulty concentrating
- Poor diet
- Fluctuating health or weight
- Negative or impulsive thoughts
- Bad stomach
- Looking forward to cocktail hour too much
- Bad reaction from your spouse
- Bad reaction from your kids
- Bad reaction from your dog

You get the idea. You cannot be a good leader, manager, or person if you are too stressed out. In the macho work world of construction, showing weakness is considered taboo. This hidden stress, frustration, and unhappiness can have a very significant impact on not only the individual but also the workplace.

Stress costs North American businesses billions of dollars per year. So this is not a little touchy-feely problem; it is a legitimate business concern. Stress and its impact on performance are bottom-line issues. As a leader, you are going to have to manage it on an ongoing basis. Ignoring is not managing it. Internalizing it is not managing it. Taking it out on your employees is not managing it. Screwing up your marriage and kids is not managing it. Requiring your employees to "suck it up" is not managing it. Am I being clear enough here?

Most health insurance offers stress-reduction programs. There are many other avenues to dealing with it. But it is a three-sided cure: physical exercise (an outlet for the physical manifestations of stress), emotional release (yes, you actually might have to talk to someone; it's your choice to pay for a professional or not), and psychological health (no, I don't think you are any crazier than anyone else I know...and everyone I know is screwed up in one way or another).

Manage stress. When it goes 360 on you, everyone else will know. Except possibly you.

PLS #8: Maintain Work-Life Balance

My dad never went to my ballgames when I was a kid, and I did not expect it. At that time fathers were absent from active involvement and engagement in their kids' lives. That has changed dramatically. Now, parents want to be involved at all levels of their kids' development and achievement. In the modern workplace this can be a difficult challenge for supervisors to handle.

From dentist appointments to soccer games to recitals, parents want to be front and center. This is especially important to those who are in the younger Generation X and Y populations, as their parents were there for them most of the time, so they have come to accept being there as standard practice. Also, many people now have the additional challenge of two-career families. The old idea that parenting was purely the job of the mom has pretty much gone by the wayside.

So how does a leader, on the frontlines of what they now call "work-life balance," try to get things done without being the insensitive guy? The easy way (but not the best) is simply to say no to everyone all the time. Since that probably does not work for you or the organization you are managing, here are some other tips for you to consider:

- You are going to be judged not just on your response to any one request but on how fair you handle all of them. By accommodating one person are you going to alienate five others? Play no favorites.

- What is the frequency for you to exercise some flexibility? Some employees are going to make assumptions about what is and is not acceptable. If you do it without going over what the limitations are, you are setting up employees to automatically expect consideration as an unofficial benefit. Anything you provide several times will not be considered a special perk but more as standard operating procedure.

- Ask for something in return. Not all the time, but asking employees for something reminds them it is not a one-way street. It reminds them they are being provided time or flexibility and that the employer deserves the same kind of extra consideration in return.

- Helping people meet their competing personal demands between work and family can pay huge dividends in terms of long-term loyalty and employee retention.

- There are always exceptions to the rule when it comes to people. I am not suggesting you violate company policies. I am suggesting that you should not get so caught up in structure and rules that you lose sight of what is reasonable. Or critical. Or human. I leave you to struggle with the gray areas by using your best judgment, logic, and empathy combined.

PLS #9: Have Fun (Sometimes)

Over sixty percent of people in the U.S. workforce report they are not happy at work. That is tens of millions of people just going through the grind every day. Those numbers do not even ask about having fun at work. Having some fun is a critical part of enjoying life and work. Promoting fun might also be a damn good leadership strategy. Work is not just about earning enough time or money to go have fun; it is about trying to enjoy what you are doing while at work (sometimes).

For me it has become more difficult to have fun as my responsibilities have increased. The magnitude of the people and business problems puts a lot of pressure on me. Being responsible for people and their families can weigh heavily. Having more problems than solutions is not the time I want to kick up my heels and sing a song. So I really have had to make a more conscious effort to be sure that fun is an ongoing part of my daily routine. A leader can end up dull and deadly serious if not. A leader can miss a lot of life in pursuit of accomplishment and also miss the benefits and camaraderie that fun and humor provide to a team.

A leader should occasionally create a dynamic of fun and enjoyment with his or her team. I personally don't like the slap-on-the-back, tell-a-joke-a-day kind of fun, but that's just me. With my teams I have done everything from chair races, to BBQs and beer, to practical jokes (some on me), to Make-A-Wish Foundation fundraising by letting industry leaders hurl pies in my face (with the help of the San Francisco 49ers cheerleaders). All of these events show the human side of everyone at work. Adding a little fun can and should be simple. It should add to morale. It should show your humor and lighter side. It does not have to cost a lot. It means a lot to your team, especially if you drive them hard. I do, so in my case it does mean a lot.

It does not matter if you are a foreman, manager, or top dog, going through life choosing work as a grind is no fun. Sometimes there is little time for it as a leader, but fun balances out the other rough times, of which there are many. Why work so hard, to rise so high, and not have fun?

CHAPTER FOUR

Alpha Manager

"Effective leadership is putting first things first. Effective management is exercising discipline in carrying it out."
—STEPHEN COVEY

Teaching and Coaching to Hit the Target

The power of teaching and coaching properly and professionally should not be underestimated. Done well, teaching has a permanent positive impact on those who are smart enough to accept it. It is a foundation for good managers seeking superior results.

It is a lesson I am working on with my daughter, Ally. A child's capacity to focus and concentrate on any one thing for any period of time is key to his or her long-term success. Socially, academically, and physically this applied lesson creates opportunity. The same applies in the construction workplace.

Once per year, Ally and I remove ourselves from the world. We escape to the backcountry up to the highest reaches of the Sierra Nevada Mountains to be on our own in a remote wilderness. We have done this since she was five years old. It is a classroom for her personal development.

What happens when there are no cell phones, no TV, no Play Stations, no distractions? How does it feel with no newspapers, no faxes, no videos, or email? The level of concentration and focus immediately rises. The resources of mind, body, and spirit are not so dissipated. There is some initial discomfort, for it is difficult to go from one extreme to the other. As well, when was the last time you were with your child twenty-four hours a day for seven days with no one else around? Truly, the concentration on parenting, coaching, teaching, and communicating is unlike anything that happens in the rush-rush parenting typical of all of our schedules.

So, when given this opportunity for greater concentration and clarity, I try to give Ally the opportunity to use our getaways in an achievement-based way. Fishing: patience. Rock climbing: focus. Animal tracks: observation. Fire starting: ingenuity. Archery: concentration. First aid: action in the face of urgency. Mountain climbing: mental and physical endurance. As I have taught these lessons, I have learned from her that concentration is a learned response from good coaching and teaching. Yes, some of us are gifted with natural capacity, but it is always something that you can culture and further develop. And when you push aside distractions or interruptions, you can see the results quickly and dramatically.

A few years ago, I taught Ally to shoot a bow and arrow. She started with it as a novel idea, but each arrow went far and wide. With initial failure, it also hurt her hand. It hurt her wrist. It was too hot. It wasn't fun. But slowly, with coaching and instruction, she came to her own internal understanding. She began to focus and to concentrate. On her own. To block out me, the environment, and her thoughts. She nailed the target. And after a few hours it was no longer the target but the bullseye. And then she took five steps back and five steps more, challenging herself, her concentration becoming the means to her success.

Business leaders and construction organizations should take heed of this lesson. The cultivation of concentration and focus as a strategic approach is a powerful tool. Coaching to not be reactive. To not be too many things to too many people. To not be spread too thin. To spend undivided time with key people. This is a rare investment of time but a very worthwhile one for a professional manager in our industry.

Finally, there is also a personal payoff for the teacher, coach, or manager. I am proud of her for learning and achieving something I probably could not have done at her age. And it is more the knowledge that she can strongly concentrate and focus on her desired outcome that makes it worth the time and the lessons learned year after year. I guess the moral to the story is that we do not always have the ability to stop all distractions or deal with only one issue at a time. We do, however, always have the choice of what we will focus on and the degree to which we are committed to the desired outcome—to hitting the target.

Managing Policy and Structure

Managing Polices, Guidelines, and the Human Element

Company policies exist to shape the workplace; they are a very important part of making the workplace fair, safe, and uniform. But policies are only words in a handbook. It is people who have to make them, follow them, and enforce them. And in this regard, a good leader and manager needs to understand how to keep the human element engaged, aligned, and intact.

Most policies are reflective of things that have gone wrong. If nothing went wrong, who would need policies? We would all just do the right things all the time, every day. Since we are all imperfect (some more than others), policies play a critical role.

Here are some basic guidelines for managing company policies:

1. Make sure everyone understands them. Many problems occur from a lack of understanding of policies. Employees are often embarrassed or afraid to ask questions about policies because they think they will be identified as potential troublemakers. I tell them it is better to ask questions now than beg forgiveness later.

2. Don't dump policy changes on employees. Make sure that when new policies are enacted everyone knows the why and when. If you ask people to follow rules and don't give them good reasons why, they will almost always assume the worst. Great policies poorly introduced can blow up in your face.

3. Remember the first question employees will think (but not ask): "How is this going to impact me personally?" It is not them being selfish; it is simply human nature. Am I getting screwed? Is this going to be a big problem? Is this more work? Remember that they are going to process it personally before they process it professionally.

4. Give a little. Some company policies cannot be compromised an inch. If they have to do with the safety and well-being of the employees and company, there is not any room for consideration. On the other hand, you will be given many situations where you will have to make a judgment call—a small matter in the "gray area" that may not be a huge deal to you or the company may be a very big deal to your employee.

Because People Will Do Stupid Things

Why do we really need the hassle of these company policies, regulations, and paperwork? Because of one of the great mysteries of management—that eventually most of your employees will do stupid things. Even some of your good ones.

Oh, there are exceptions to every rule. And on a stupid factor of 1–10 most people will rarely get above a five. But rather than drive yourself crazy asking why people do such things, you have to learn to accept this fact and find ways to reduce or eliminate repetitive patterns of poor judgment. Approaching situations this way takes your personal judgment and the emotion that comes with it out of your resolution process. That is not to say every situation can be met calmly and with grace.

In my years of top management have I ever yelled at an employee? Yes, guilty as charged. Above a stupid factor of eight, it is really hard to hold back. Have I ever thrown anything around my office? Yes. Maximum frustration at a nine can have that effect. Have I ever smashed down a phone so hard that it needed to be replaced?

Ummm, that's enough about me and my great management abilities. Let's just say that sometimes people will do or say things that are so astoundingly foolish, dishonest, hurtful, unsafe, or malicious that your "pissed off" animal response might get ahead of your best leadership instincts. The fact that people go haywire with some regularity is surprising to some but should be anticipated by a top leader. Aside from those crazy one in ten thousand events, it is up to you to handle the worst that people can throw at you with reason and maturity.

Establishing The Line

A manager in any organization is no longer "one of the guys." Managers have different responsibilities. You have a higher degree of accountability. You are where the buck stops. And that is why you and your subordinates have to have a very clear understanding of "The Line."

What is "The Line"? It is the clear boundary between friendship and business decisions. It is the unspoken but understood fact that members of your team cannot use a personal relationship with them to assume anything. I tell you this from first-hand experience and a lot of heartache. You cannot be a good manager or leader without The Line. You must draw it yourself; your employees won't. You must define its limits and parameters. But don't think you can jump back and forth across it because the bottom line is, you can't.

Many leaders want to be buddies with their employees. They want to have fun or go drinking or socialize off hours—and all that is fine. But be aware that if you have no Line, your employees (when they need or want something) are going to be looking at you as their "friend" and not their "supervisor." They are going to be expecting to be treated as a "friend" with all the flexibility and consideration that comes with it. If you give them anything less it becomes personal to them—and right there The Line becomes blurry. A blurry Line will cause you no end of trouble.

The Line Is Never Blurry

Managers must know that The Line between them and their teams is never blurry. This is a very difficult concept to follow, but you need to make sure you never waver. If you are wondering if your Line is blurry, answer some of these questions honestly:

- Do you drink or socialize with your employees outside of work? If so, do you act differently than you do at work?
- Have you ever interacted with employees in a way that could detract from your role as respected and trustworthy leader?
- Do your employees see you as a respected leader or a friend of theirs who just happens to be in charge?
- How does that perception color their performance and their expectations of how you should treat them?
- Do you have some personal friends on your team while others are just your subordinates? Do you think that discrepancy appears confusing to some in the workplace?
- Are there perceptions of leaders "playing favorites" within your organization or your team?
- When you have to criticize or discipline employees, how do they take it—personally or professionally? Might it depend on their perception of the relationship between them and you?

No matter what you think, the minute people working for you believe they are your friend first and employee second, they will expect you to cut them slack even if they doesn't deserve it. The person will expect you to understand and adapt to their personal problems and circumstances. He or she will take everything personally, and that will be reflected in his or her work performance.

Do not let The Line get blurry. Does this mean you have to be stuck up and distant? Not at all. In fact, you should have a relationship that is friendly, supportive, interactive, and real. But work always has to come first. The organizational mission and objectives have to be foremost. Any compromises you make are only for your benefit and comfort. You want it easier? You want to play favorites? You want to be liked as a buddy? Sorry, but you can't have it both ways.

Don't Be "The Hub"

This is a lesson in management structure. At one time or another, by design or mistake, most leaders become "The Hub." The Hub, as illustrated by the diagram below, represents the typical way teams, businesses, or organizations are often led and managed. In The Hub model, everyone brings everything to a central person. The Hub system of leadership holds back both people and organizations.

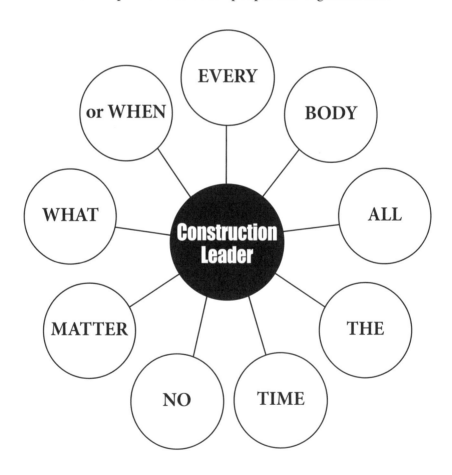

The most frequent cause of The Hub is when an organization grows or the leader moves to a higher position and their methodology of management does not change. The small team Hub methodology becomes replicated in larger applications. And it usually fails both the leader and the organization.

Do you have a Hub problem? Ask yourself these questions to find out:

- Was the leadership structure of your organization planned, or did it evolve? (If it just evolved, you can be sure you have The Hub somewhere.)
- Did anyone explain to you in detail how decisions are made in your organization and what is expected of you in this regard? (If not, then people are making it up as they go along—and this is Hub behavior.)
- Does your leadership structure maximize delegation? (If not, you have Hub leaders hoarding tasks or decisions or, worse, still trying to do their last job too.)
- Are you encountering problems involving overlap or confusion of responsibilities? (These are symptoms of non-integrated Hub management systems.)

If you are wondering whether The Hub has an operational or economic impact on your team or the organization, then check and see if any of these symptoms apply:

- How much time do leaders spend firefighting (as opposed to doing the most important things that create the most opportunities)?
- Do people regularly come to supervisors for answers to problems or questions they should be handling themselves?
- Can people go around others to get the answers they want?
- Can people jump the chain of command for personal or petty reasons?
- Do you have disruptive office politics?

If you answered yes to any of these questions, it might be time to review the organizational structure of your team or organization. But as you try to change the structure or people in it, you need to consider the obstacles you are facing. There are powerful motivations on why people lead or manage from the center of The Hub. Most of the reasons are ones we never think of. The Hub generally exists for the following reasons:

- The leader likes it that way. There is a big payoff for being at the center. The main payoffs are feeling important, being needed, or having control.
- The Hub just evolved, so no one even thinks about it. Change seems unnecessary.
- It is a family business; therefore, the patriarch or matriarch is at the center but not for good business reasons.
- There are poorly defined lines of responsibility and authority and probably no job descriptions or organizational charts.
- The business calls itself a family and wants to pretend it is. Just a reminder—families are bonded by love. Businesses are bonded by results.
- Poor delegators stay in The Hub.
- Control freaks stay in The Hub.
- Organizational politicians promote their own Hub.
- Those who try to give up The Hub are often worried about what they are going to do next.

The Hub teaches poor practices. The Hub limits growth. The Hub is fine for very small enterprises only. Act accordingly.

Processes Dictate Results

In many organizations the management and leadership approach is to hire talented people and turn them loose. The assumption is that if you hire talented people, you shouldn't have to tell them what to do or how to do it. As a result, they don't spend too much time refining their processes and systems. In the construction industry, people and companies like to build projects but are far less enthused about building the internal infrastructure and systems of an organization. It is not as fun. It is not as interesting. It does not seem to pay the bills. It is often an area of weakness for senior management. It is usually an area of weakness for field managers. This is a short-sighted and undisciplined approach. Well-defined processes and systems get stuff accomplished. And whether they are formal or informal, processes and systems always dictate results.

A lot of organizations don't see the value of developing systems and processes. Construction likes its rough-and-tumble image. So systems are left for the bean counters and computer people and other cubicle dwellers. Systems seem too formal and involve too much paperwork and bureaucracy. These excuses allow leaders to leave process to chance and to accept inconsistent and unpredictable results. Also, a lack of emphasis on process does not give individuals or organizations the opportunity to improve. Organizations without uniform processes and effective systems find it difficult to:

- Measure results
- Evaluate costs or people in a timely manner
- Maintain standards
- Train new employees effectively
- Cross train employees between departments, field and office
- Replace intellectual capital lost when employees leave
- Assist managers with utilizing best practices
- Engage employees in suggested process improvements
- Evaluate the potential of individuals and teams accurately
- Reach best practice standards

This is a lesson I learned the hard way. I was a "get-it-done" kind of leader for a long time. Process did not interest me and sometimes just seemed to get in the way. I, like most Alphas, was just interested in results. My attitude was: Give me the bottom line. I don't care how you get there; just get there. But with every changing face in the organization we had to start over. You see, if you lack structure and process, you are depending on the intellectual capital of your employees. They have the knowledge of processes locked up inside them instead of at the disposal of the organization. What does this do?

- It means every time you lose an employee you also lose the organizational process history.
- It means that no one actually has a clear idea of exactly how things are supposed to be done.
- It means that most every new guy is going to reinvent the wheel and waste time and money.
- And it is twice as difficult to analyze or improve any process if it is not clearly defined and, typically, put in writing.

Understanding organizational processes, being able to describe them clearly, being able to use them to train people for existing or new positions, and utilizing them to leverage organizational assets better are all essentials for good leaders and managers. A focus on process creates greater efficiencies, higher productivity, less waste, and higher profits or market share.

I know there are many people who are going to say they don't need process to make them successful. And they are right. They need process to make their organization successful—even if they don't like it or are not good at it.

Sanity, Productivity, and Time Management

There are many courses on time management as well as many systems you can buy. I strongly suggest you do a lot more learning about this very important subject. Time management can be as formal or informal as you want; but, for sure, if you have no reliable method, then you are likely being reactive. This means that on a day-to-day or even a minute-by-minute basis you are letting the circumstances around you set your time investment priorities. Bad idea. No matter how good you get at leading with this approach, you will be nothing more than a highly skilled firefighter, jumping from hot spot to hot spot but missing the key overall priorities you need to establish within your own timeframes.

Here are six time-management strategies for you to consider, loosely based on recommendations from the Mayo Clinic, one of the premier medical facilities in the U.S. Why a medical clinic as a source? Because time management is also one of the best ways to reduce stress and thus improve your health, if not your sanity.

- Plan, plan, plan your time in writing.
- Prioritize all your key tasks daily and weekly.
- Delegate. Make sure you are doing the tasks best suited for your position and responsibility. This is a real killer for people who like to "do things" more than they like to plan and monitor progress. It is also a big problem for new managers and leaders.
- Limit distractions. Don't check your cell phone or email every few minutes. Don't return every voice mail or text message immediately. Don't train yourself to have the attention span of a duck.
- Break big tasks into smaller segments. When you break up the time projects take into manageable chunks, you often find that the sequence and outcome are much smoother. It also reduces procrastination.
- Say no. Say no to obligations or time drags that do not contribute to what you are trying to get done. Don't let guilt, obligation, or the word "yes" kill your productivity.

Planning: The 2:1 Payback

Many construction field leaders are weak at planning. For many construction field leaders, planning is not "doing." Action means movement. Action means production. For some it is better to be in motion even if you are figuring it out as you go along. That is not being a professional leader, though. That is often a sign of being impatient and disorganized.

To understand the real value of planning, consider that every minute invested in it yields approximately twice as much time saved in terms of productivity—and thus increased profits. Remember the old saying, "Measure twice, cut once"?

You would never see a football team go on the field without a play. Teams spend hours in the classroom watching films and practicing before they execute. That play defines the who, what, where, when, and why. Everyone understands their role. Everyone is aligned. The outcome and objective are clear. And everyone is therefore responsible. In our construction industry, planning ahead is sometimes just a moment-to-moment thing. Or the supervisor directs activity instead of executing a plan. The workers then are just acting on command rather than understanding the big picture. They may be ready and willing, but without the plan they are stuck waiting on the next instruction. Lack of planning also starts to show up as problems such as these:

- Lack of materials or tools to do the job
- Wrong materials or tools to do the job
- Materials or tools not placed in proper locations for maximum productivity
- Work flow not predetermined
- Missed opportunities to refine a plan of construction from estimate
- Excessive waste

- Poor coordination with the owner or other sub-contractors
- Project is over-manned or under-manned
- Poor documentation or paperwork
- Safety shortcuts or compromises
- Ineffective field cost control
- A moment-to-moment management style also known as firefighting

These days the regular use of software programs like Primavera deal with the construction schedule, but there are at least a half-dozen other areas that need the same detailed planning to maximize production. There is such a thing as too much planning, and I have known project engineers and inspectors who have the "paralysis from analysis" gene. But they are rare in comparison to those who combine their drive and determination with winging it.

Planning takes discipline. Planning is its own activity. Leaders and managers must be encouraged to take the time to do it. It is not "dead time." It is the key to a 2:1 productivity payback.

Managing Talent

Non-Pro Managers = Loss of Talent and Money

Alpha managers need to be professional, especially if they have a blue collar. People are the most valuable part of any construction business plan, and handling the talent has the greatest impact on the bottom line.

On the other hand, non-professional management is a very expensive problem. It is not always visible, but it is as bad as having someone skim from your organization's bank account. What is the primary cost impact to most organizations? The number one impact reported as a result of poor supervision is loss of key talent. The costs associated with loss of talent are lost time, training, knowledge, momentum, growth opportunity, and peer performance. And that's just the beginning.

In various national workplace surveys thirty percent of employees report no confidence in their direct supervisor. A University of Tallahassee study of ten thousand workplaces indicated that more than forty percent of supervisors are not properly trained or competent. On the other hand, the number one factor for job satisfaction is an employee's relationship with his or her direct supervisor. So the real question is: Do highly talented and valuable people quit working for a company or for a bad boss?

- People quit when they are not respected. When respect is not the currency that passes between boss and subordinate, manipulation can become the norm.
- People quit untrustworthy people. If integrity is compromised, employee morale goes down immediately.
- Employees quit incompetent bosses. Productivity and momentum hit the highway.
- People quit bosses who have "issues."
- People quit bosses who won't invest in them because they see them as a threat, not an opportunity.
- People quit bosses who do not see or address their blind spots.
- People quit unprofessional people when they can work for professionals someplace else.

Managing Like Socrates

Managing like a pro is not really so tough. Let's take our first lesson from Socrates. Socrates was a wise sage and teacher who lived more than two thousand years ago. His legacy, which lives on today, is the method he used to teach. The Socratic Method teaches by asking questions. Socrates challenged his students by asking them questions that stimulated their thinking and reasoning. From first grade through college success is often based on your ability to retain material and then regurgitate it on a test at a later date. This method does not always teach people to reason. It does not challenge people to think or analyze as they might. And most of all it does not refine their judgment. Teaching by asking questions helps in all these areas, and I have adopted this as a primary method of both training and leading because it works great.

I learned this lesson from another of my successful construction mentors. When I was younger, I used to go around to his jobsites with him. I noted that he constantly asked open-ended questions. From the lowest guy on the jobsite to the top managers, he treated them all the same, with a sincere, down-home inquiry (though I am sure he already knew most of the answers they were going to give him anyway). What I saw in return is that they did not fear him. They did not give him "yes-man" answers. On his side he was listening very closely to what they had to offer. He built his company on this approach and value system. He instilled a culture of participation. Since he had seven hundred employees, I guess his approach must have worked.

When you're looking for information, problem-solving opportunities, or anything else from your team, ask open-ended questions. Open-ended questions cannot be answered with a yes or a no.

Socrates might have made a hell of an Alpha if he'd wanted because his method can work at your business to engage people every day. So let's look at specific open-ended questions you can ask—if you've got the guts to hear the answers—that will give you valuable content:

- What are we doing just because we've always done it?
- What took too long?
- What should we change now?
- What would you have done instead?
- What am I missing?
- Why do you think that happened?

- What do you think he was thinking?
- What caused complaints (internally or externally)?
- What cost too much?
- What was wasted?
- What job involved too many people?
- What could be simplified?
- What was misunderstood?
- What should we never change?
- What did you learn?

I ask that last question all the time. It frustrates people the first fifty times you ask it, but it is one question that has paid more dividends than any other I have ever asked in my professional career.

A lot of leaders miss this opportunity by "directing" instead of "asking." There is a time for direction and a time for obtaining input. I tend to be a very impatient person, so it is very hard for me to slow down long enough to take my own advice, but I am never sorry when I do. Finally, when you ask these questions of your team, what are you telling them?

- I want and respect your opinion.
- I believe you have something to contribute.
- This is a team effort.
- I care about your participation.
- I want you to think for yourself.
- You can trust me. I trust you.

Failing to Listen

I have never excelled at listening. It is a problem for a lot of people who are leaders. We are too busy telling people what to do, what we think, or what they are doing wrong. So take it from a lousy listener, there is real potential here. What are the primary obstacles to good listening? Here are a few I'm familiar with:

- I can't listen if I am telling you what to do.
- I can't listen if I am thinking about something while you are talking.
- I can't listen if I am thinking about my response while you are still talking.
- I can't listen if I am interrupting you three times per conversation.
- I can't listen patiently when it seems like you are telling me your entire (boring) life story, but I only want to know about issues, facts, or problems.
- I can't listen if I don't regularly extend courtesy and respect to others.
- I can't listen well if as soon as I hear something I don't agree with I stop listening.

What are the consequences of not listening well?
- I don't get the details I need to make a good decision as a leader.
- I convey lack of respect.
- I don't hear about ideas for improvement.
- When others can see I'm not listening, they will stop talking. Sometimes when they need to the most.
- A leader who listens poorly teaches others to listen poorly.

Choosing Delegation vs. DIY

Effective delegation can be one of the most difficult skills of an effective leader. This is especially difficult if you used to do the job that your team members are now doing. Delegation obstacles you are likely to encounter might include:

- Do It Yourself (DIY) Syndrome: You know how to do it, and it seems easier to do it because it will save time and effort. Actually, you are retarding your team's development and limiting their capacity to earn your trust.

- I Can't Wait All Day: This obstacle occurs when you do not have the patience to let your team members do what you have delegated to them. They initially will take longer than you want them to or need them to. But the more you delegate, the more they advance their learning curve, and the faster they will accomplish the tasks. By delegating to them and then placing unrealistic time periods on their accomplishment, you set both them and yourself up for failure.

- Piece by Piece: Instead of delegating the project, you delegate tasks that lead to accomplishment of the desired outcome bit by bit, which often leads to…

- Over the Shoulder: You say you are delegating but in reality lack the trust or vision to allow someone else to accomplish the task independently. You watch over the person's shoulder and interfere in the task.

- Second-Guessing Picasso: You don't hire Picasso and then tell him what to paint. If you are not capable of delegating work, then you are either failing to develop the people you hired to accept additional responsibility or you hired the wrong people to begin with. In summary, if you can't delegate, it's probably your fault.

Seven Tips for Effective Delegation

Delegation is the key to advancement. If you can't find effective ways to move things off your plate and onto others', you cannot advance. If you can't delegate in a manner that leverages the talent of those around you, then you can't advance. If you hoard tasks and responsibilities because you like them, have always done them, or are afraid to let go, then you can't advance either. So here are seven strategies to delegate well:

1. Be clear in identifying the desired outcome, including the deadline.

2. Be clear with your original directions. Do not assume they can or will fill in the blanks.

3. If necessary, make them write down key details. Sometimes people are too embarrassed to take the notes they will need an hour, day, or week later.

4. Ask them if they have any questions before they engage in the task. This saves both you and them time.

5. Tell them they can come for help if necessary. But if they encounter a problem in execution, tell them not to bring you a problem only but at least one alternative to solve it. Otherwise, you create a dependent workplace culture where thinking for one's self is not encouraged or required.

6. Delegation frequently leads to mistakes. Analyze the mistake. Avoid blaming. Determine whether a mistake is someone else's fault or your own. That's right. Yours. If you did not help someone understand a task, timeline, technical aspects, or other vital information, how can you expect that person to succeed? If it is the employee's mistake find out how it was made. Does he or she have a skill deficiency? Poor analytical or judgment skills? A lack of confidence? An inability to obtain the buy-in of others? Spend the time *this time* so that the problem is unlikely to occur *next time*.

7. Praise accomplishment. Delegation has a payoff for you and them. You don't have to do the tasks, and employees get ownership of a positive outcome. Let them know if they did well. For many people that is the best motivation for taking on more responsibilities next time.

Micromanaging

Except for the drunken abusive smelly incompetent stupid unethical jerk, a micromanager control freak is everyone's next least favorite person to work for. Micromanagement is exactly what it sounds like: someone consumed with controlling all the little tasks of his or her subordinates. Micromanagers are also often ineffective and under perform because of their control issues.

There are many leaders and managers who have huge control issues. Sometimes people rise in their organizations because of them. Unfortunately, micromanagement guarantees that:

- The employees being supervised are going to be frustrated.
- The work will generally take longer to complete.
- The creativity and innovation that comes from collaboration will be lost.
- Employees will be reduced to task-level thinking.
- Errors will be fewer but initiative and risk-taking behavior will be at a minimum.
- No one is learning anything on his or her own.
- Most employees are seriously fantasizing about throwing the micromanager in front of a semi.

If you are wondering whether you are a micromanager or whether you are working with or for one, here are some danger signs. A micromanager:

- Tells you what to do, tells you how to do it, and watches you do it
- Exhibits hypercritical behavior regarding small parts of projects or tasks
- Needs excessive reports or feedback at all-too-frequent intervals
- Provides resistance or hostility to any changes in process or procedure even if results are better
- Is rigid and controlling in personality or communications
- Does not do his or her own job while doing all of the above
- And on top of all this, he or she jumps in to do the tasks because of an inability to stand having them done any other way

Micromanagement does not bring out the best in people. Control freakism is a personal issue that someone is working out at the expense of others. Micromanagement exists in organizations where it is allowed to exist. If you see the signs in yourself or subordinates, a major change is in order. If your boss has multiple signs of the above, a change in employment is in order. You will never grow personally or professionally while working for a micromanager; don't trade your long-term potential for a paycheck.

Finally, if you have this problem, be assured it is your problem. It is not that your employees are too stupid to do without your insecure control freak hovering bullshit. Take this simple advice: Focus on results, not details. Focus on results, not details. Focus on results, not details.

Hiring and Interviewing: Three Key Elements

Over the years I have probably interviewed close to five hundred candidates for different positions. Some were a pleasure, some were not, and some were just weird. Until you've interviewed someone who puts their elbows on your desk while smacking their gum or have had someone give one-word answers through gritted teeth while avoiding eye contact, you really haven't lived. The mini-drama of interviewing people (and hopefully hiring) is one of the most high-value activities that a leader can engage in. Not everyone reading this book is in a position (yet) to be interviewing and hiring, but those opportunities and challenges might be just around the corner. So here are three things for you to think about regarding hiring and interviews:

1. *Obtaining Core Information*

What are the purposes of an interview? The most obvious one might be determining whether a person is right for the job. But in reality you want core information on the person and not just his or her qualifications. Here are a few additional qualities that nearly every hiring decision has to cover:

- Is the person qualified by experience and/or education?
- Has the applicant done his or her homework on the company?
- Can the person think on his or her feet?
- Does he or she display confidence and independence?
- Does the chemistry feel right?
- Does the person have questions that indicate a sincere interest in and keen understanding of the opportunity?
- Does the interview give you an example of how the person might perform under stress?
- Does the applicant know whether he or she really wants the job?
- Does the prospective employee have realistic expectations?

2. *Getting Married after the First Date*

Suffice it to say that interviews are very important but also very superficial. They are like getting married after the first date. You meet with someone an hour or maybe two. Then you can end up working with the person for forty to fifty hours a week for three to five to ten years. How much sense is there in that? Not much—but it is the standard of our industry, so let's figure out how to get the most out of it. If you are going to marry someone that fast, here are a few things you need to moderate in your interview and hiring process:

- Personal chemistry: Don't hire someone because you like him or her. Ideally, you will like the person you hire a lot, but that should not be the primary reason.

- Instinct or gut: You cannot ignore your feelings about a candidate, but hiring someone based only on those is a roll of the dice.

- Qualifications: I have had many employees who were supremely qualified. I hired them for that. I fired them for the same reason. It was all they had to offer.

- In your own image: Don't hire in your own image. Let me give you an example of what I'm talking about: I am terribly frustrated by people who need to go over minute details. Like I need to hear about ten thousand years of history to order some pencils! Some people think that if something is important to them, it must also be important to me. But to have an excellent organization, sometimes you have to hire people who are the exact opposite of you. That kind of balance in talent and temperament is very important. Everyone is not supposed to be like you.
- Conformance and compliance: Don't look for vanilla. Don't look for people trying to give you the right answers. Look for people giving you their real answers. An honest response is much better than a well coached one.
- Watch for small red flags: If you see something even tiny that rubs you the wrong way, pay attention to it.

3. ***Their Best Day Five Years from Now***

When you are interviewing a potential candidate for any job, remember that you are looking at the person on his or her absolute best day. This is as good as it gets. Therefore, any small concerns you may have are likely to be houses on fire in a year.

Checking References: Getting to the Meth Habit

The reference check is a mandatory verification that is part of protecting the interests of your organization and your direct team. Many organizations skip it and pay the price. My take is that eighty percent of references are totally worthless. Applicants are providing these references because they know they are going to get a great review. Fine. What I want to know about is their secret meth habit, their ax-murderer tendencies, or sixty-one days they called in sick last year. When I call to find out about someone, I want to know whether he or she has a fatal flaw.

Usually, when I call a reference, the person tells me how the applicant is the most amazing human being on the planet and the most responsible and how lucky I will be to hire him or her. I tell the reference how impressive all of that sounds. I also say it looks like I am going to hire the person. At that moment I have let the reference off the hook. The job he or she is performing is done—almost. Then I bring up the Fatal Flaw inquiry, and it sounds like this:

> *Hey, when I bring so-and-so aboard, what should I really focus on helping him or her with right away? I need a successful employee, so what would you suggest I really do to help this person improve in one key area?*

When the reference thinks the person is basically hired, he or she will be honest with you. And then you will find out whether there is a Fatal Flaw. The reference will tell you what you need to know. I cannot tell you how many times the answer defined a hiring decision. I have obtained information about problems with attitude, follow though, teamwork, self-esteem, and lack of skill sets. In summary, when checking references, forget the praise and fluff and look for the Fatal Flaw.

Hiring and Firing (Psychotic) Rabid Dogs

There will come a time, if it has not come already, when you will hire an employee who at first seems to shine with potential. The person will seem to have everything you need. And this is the problem. Your need is blinding you to a terrible and painful fate that lies ahead of you: the problem of the psychotic rabid dog.

These people are usually very charismatic, friendly, and seemingly straightforward. They might at first seem to get along with people and have a great personality. But just under the surface lies an entirely different person. People such as this are deeply flawed from an emotional or psychological standpoint. When they are under the least amount of pressure, they begin to show it in their interactions with other employees, customers, and you. They can be liars. They can be game players. They can be thieves. They can be workplace politicians or assassins. They can look you in the eye and lie, cheat, or steal. They foam at the mouth, but it is hard to see because they hide it well. Want one case study?

Fifteen years ago Joe was one of my managers. He was a great guy. Everyone really liked him. He was funny and charming. He did his job well. But he was a Bad Dog. He got a DUI and didn't tell us. He puked in the company car. He bought Giants tickets with company funds. He lied, cheated, and stole. And I missed it. I fired him but felt like firing myself. I should have focused more on him. I took my eye off the ball because he was a good guy and I was busy and a bunch of other lousy reasons and excuses. He was a psycho liar, and I should have seen it and done something about it at least six months earlier. Nice doggy, yeah right. Years later I'm still mad at myself.

These people can cause more grief in a shorter time period than anyone you can possibly imagine. Over twenty-five years I have had at least three of them sneak in on me (despite three rounds of interviews). I hired and subsequently fired them. The clean-up period for each ranged from weeks to many months. It was always expensive.

So be careful. Never let your organizational needs or a promising personality blind you to someone's true nature. Believe me, once you've been there you will know that some psycho employees really should be institutionalized or just shot down like Old Yeller.

Providing Feedback and Evaluations

Feedback and evaluations are very important for employees even if they are sometimes a time-consuming pain in the butt for the manager or leader. But proper evaluations and feedback are absolutely essential for many employees to feel valued. Let me relate a story that illustrates the importance of providing good feedback.

Ten years ago I was interviewing candidates for an executive assistant position. I was not looking for someone to answer the phone and shuffle my papers. I was looking for a high-level professional who could keep up with my Alpha drive, determination, and high-energy personality. In the midst of the process I interviewed an outstanding candidate who had been the executive assistant to three Fortune 1000 CEOs. She had everything: poise, class, brains, diplomacy. She was also making great money—so why the hell is she looking to work for me?

I asked her why she was leaving her great position, and the first reason was that her boss never gave her any feedback. Never gave her any evaluations. Simply put, she didn't know where she stood. Now, he probably thought that her salary told her. Or maybe he just didn't value feedback. But it cost him one of the best executive assistants in the U.S. I hired her, and ten years later I make damn sure she knows where she stands.

There are many people like this in the workplace starving for constructive feedback and evaluations and an equal number of leaders, managers, and foremen who think they are too busy to make them a priority. It does not matter whether the person is an apprentice or a journeyman or a senior estimator. People need feedback to improve. People need feedback to benchmark their performance. People need feedback for their self-esteem. People need feedback for morale. People also need evaluations so they can put together plans for self-improvement. It is a business tool that construction ignores because we assume people "just know." It is especially important to anyone who is thirty-five years old or younger as they indicate in every employment survey that they want weekly and even daily feedback. Yes, it is very time-consuming, but if you don't give employees what they need, they are not going to produce at the level they are capable of.

Take the time to give people feedback, and make sure it is balanced. In construction we are very quick to tell people what they did wrong but far less likely to recognize what was done well. And give feedback at reasonable intervals. I make sure everyone in my organization gets a chance to discuss their performance two times per year. It is about an hour each time. A mid-year check-in is informal. An end-of-year evaluation is formal and in writing.

Many companies among my clients have taught these feedback skills to their foremen and even implemented formal systems of evaluation for everyone from CEO to the newest apprentice. It is no mistake that these companies grow faster and make more money than their competitors. Providing feedback is a smart business strategy because if everyone knows where they are on the performance curve, it is easier to build a high-performance culture. Where leaders think it is unnecessary to do so or are too busy to engage in it, the talent under them may under perform or even seek new employment opportunities. Build feedback into your regular organizational and jobsite routine. It pays.

Promoting Change Strategies and the 20-60-20

Every great organization has to embrace and promote change continuously. Anything less is an organizational death sentence. Most organizations fail for the simple reason that they cannot change fast enough to meet the needs of the market. And despite all the common whining, complaining, and organizational headaches that come with change, it is important for everyone to remember that the market doesn't give a shit what you think. It only rewards you for what you do. Thus, we come to the rule of 20-60-20. These numbers are good to keep in mind when you are trying to change anything. New procedures? New structure? New technologies? New market? New service model? New pricing? New employee policies? New game plan? It's going to be 20-60-20 every time.

These numbers represent a rough statistical breakdown of the responses you will get from any group when you are trying to introduce any change initiatives. They break down as follows:

- The top twenty percent will see the operational or financial benefit to the direction you are trying to go. They will willingly and enthusiastically start acting on it right away. They are eager for change and seek new ways to do things on their own as well. These are the drivers of innovation and production in your company.

- The bottom twenty percent will fight you all the way. They resist or reject change. They stall and whine. They don't like anything that does not resemble the status quo. They remind everyone how great it was "back in the day." They have seen change initiatives come and go and figure this is just another flavor of the week. Often they will wage low-level opposition by playing internal politics to slow change down or kill it. They won't change until forced to or forced out.

- The middle sixty percent is waiting to see which of the two other groups wins.

These numbers determine the group norms on your crew or in your organization. These groups will battle for the future of your organization. It is important to remember, though, that oftentimes it is not the twenty percent resisting who keep your organization, team, or crew from going forward; it is the sixty percent who are not energized or have not bought in to a sufficient degree to move the entire organization forward.

My leadership advice? Focus on the sixty percent. The top doesn't need much additional assistance to embrace change. The bottom twenty percent is going to fight you anyway. If you can help tilt the middle sixty percent your way, you are far ahead of the game. Too many leaders spend too much time on the bottom, and it is mostly wasted effort without operational or economic return.

Finally, if you have always been a top twenty percenter, accept my sincere compliments. May you always be successful at leading necessary and constructive change. If you are generally part of the middle sixties, it is time to think about stepping up to a more proactive role. Sixty percenters cannot lead from a neutral or safe spot of non-commitment. And if you are in the bottom twenty percent, what the hell are you doing with this book in your hands? Oh, someone made you read it…(and you think it's a bunch of $%^#@*…).

(Not) Working around the Square Peg

Leadership requires constant assessment of all the people within an organization. Many leaders instead stop assessing long-term employees. They figure that employees who are launched and doing the job need little tending to. Though such employees may be lower maintenance, they still need serious assessment on an ongoing basis. Let me explain why.

In most organizations there are people who were originally fine in their jobs for the time, place, and position when they were hired. But as the company grew and changed, these employees did not. They continued to do the job but over time became less able to perform to new performance criteria, industry challenges, or workplace changes. You may have tried to help them adapt, but they were either unable or unwilling. They are now the proverbial square pegs in round holes.

As you grow as a leader and manager, you will face few challenges as difficult as this one. Such employees were possibly key players who helped you get to where you are today. Their loyalty and support were very important. Here lies the dilemma: What to do with these square pegs? What many leaders will do out of obligation and long-term loyalty is to work around them. And this, unfortunately, is not always best.

As an organization changes, those within it must change also or they will begin to feel tremendous discomfort. It is obvious to them that changes are occurring, and sometimes holding onto what they know or what is comfortable is their only way of feeling secure. The more change or responsibility passed down to them, the tighter they hold to the old ways. Beyond this, it is inevitable that others will rise and pass them in responsibility and importance. This leads to resentment, discouragement, or poor morale that can be passed on to others around them. It also becomes obvious to those who do fit into the future of your organization who these people are. They are looking to you to define what kind of organization it is you are running. Your loyalty is worthy and noble. Your willingness to take care of those who took care of you is important. But working around the square peg does send a message to everyone else that you are maintaining the status quo.

These are not easy decisions, but they are essential ones. We are talking about adaptability and flexibility. We are talking about looking ahead and not behind. Recognize that a work-around solution always has a limited time period. Recognize that the outcome might be the same, just later on. Recognize that you may have to choose between your personal feelings and the interests of your organization. No matter what decision you make, know why you made it and the impact it will have. Don't think you can do it on a situation-by-situation basis, because you can't build a winning organization with exceptions to every rule.

Promoting Employee Growth: From Poopy Diapers to Big Boy Pants

There is a time in a baby's life when you have to change his or her diapers. Why? Because babies can't do it for themselves. But wouldn't it seem odd for someone to be changing a kid's diapers when he or she is, say, twelve years old? Uh. Yeah. Gross.

Here is the same thing at work: If you allow yourself to be sucked into giving your employees solutions to every issue and challenge they face, you are just changing one more stinky diaper. Your job as leader and manager is to get them to do it for themselves. It's really difficult because being the "answer man" makes us feel important. We feel needed and powerful as a result of our knowledge.

Ideally, you have to accept the frustration that comes with knowing it is going to take longer and result in some mistakes—that sometimes when you think employees are ready for Big Boy Pants, they are going to drop a load on you. And it is so easy for you to just jump in. It is so much faster for you just to save them. You must break the habit of doing it yourself. If you want to grow in your own capacity and ability, you have to get employees to grasp the necessity and struggle of independent problem-solving. That is how they get their Big Boy Pants.

Building a Diversity Culture (at the Cowboy Bar)

There are a lot of ways to look at diversity and issues of race, gender, and creed in the construction workplace. For a leader, diversity is mostly about creating an environment in which the group (rather than the leader or company policies) dictates norms of tolerance, acceptance, and exemplary behavior. Let me share a surprising leadership story about diversity and group norms.

Kennedy Meadows is a tiny dot on the California map located seven thousand feet up in the Sierra Nevada Mountains. It's an old lodge, horse-packing station, and working ranch amid towering pines and granite peaks. As I noted previously, I have taken my daughter on an annual horse-packing trip from Kennedy Meadows into the mountains since she was five. Even now, when she's a teenager, we both still look forward to the isolation and companionship. But last year, the night before we packed out, we heard a loud disturbance coming from the rickety bar. Upon our return we heard the story behind it.

That night, in that crowded mountain cowboy bar, was a lone African-American man from the city. I don't know if I am stereotyping, but I expect most mountain cowboy bars are filled with crew cuts, rednecks and shit kickers. This one is no exception, except that some of the cowboys were Hispanic as well. It happened that one bar patron took exception to the African-American guy being there. He expressed his opinion loudly. He did so repeatedly. And then there was a little conference of the cowboys and others in the bar. And one or more of them went over and gave the man a very direct message about diversity and tolerance. Apparently, he did not get the message.

The hospital report noted that this guy had a broken arm, broken nose, cracked ribs, and various scrapes and contusions. What it should have included was that the diversity message had been delivered.

In talking to a couple of the cowboys (who weren't there…in fact, it turns out no one had been there when the sheriff came to investigate), I found the message was very simple. White rednecks and Mexican cowhands and everyone else said the same thing. They told me, "Mark, we just don't treat people that way." Even out in the boonies. Even with different races, creeds, colors, and social groups. There was no policy. It was, to them, about treating people with respect. It was about doing the right thing.

Now, I am not suggesting that racists, bigots, and harassers be taken out and beaten like a rug (unless you are absolutely sure you can get away with it). What I am suggesting is that a group norm can exist anywhere. It can exist among groups that usually don't cooperate. But the leader must set the tone of tolerance and mutual support. The leader must create an environment where certain behavior is simply not tolerated. A leader must leave no question of the company policy, the ethical line, and the moral obligation people need to have to each other.

Running a Good Meeting

Most meetings, especially in the informal environment of the construction business, don't have enough structure. As a result, the people in the meetings do too much talking and too little deciding. This is especially important on the jobsite. It is not that employees are not smart and capable; it is that the meeting process is too loose and is generally dominated by the stronger personalities.

Ninety percent of all the meetings I have ever attended were poorly run. Many were a complete waste of time. As a result, the time and talent of every person was not maximized.

The challenge of running a good meeting is to harness everyone's talent in a time-effective manner. If the leader remains focused on time, content, structure, and format, you get a far better result. Most importantly, the leader needs to be a meeting facilitator, not the lead participant. By facilitating a structured and tight meeting format and structure, the leader creates the following benefits:

- Everyone gets much more disciplined and focused in their communication.

- People used to dominating discussions have to learn patience and listening.

- People who usually tell a long story or who get bogged down in detail have to process and communicate much more quickly and effectively.

- The process eliminates personal criticism and encourages more openness and trust.

- Participants definitely get better and faster at it.

- It becomes an excellent training ground for young leaders to see how others think, analyze, and process information.

- No one goes off on time-wasting tangents.

Some helpful reminders for running an effective, productive, outcome-driven meeting are as follows:

- If there are people attending who don't know each other, have everyone introduce themselves.
- Tell the team at the meeting what the purpose of the meeting is. It seems obvious, but it helps focus people on the specific outcome.
- Don't allow anyone to go off subject. Hold anything new or unrelated to the end and deal with it only if time permits.
- Set a time to begin and end and stick to it. Late starts and meetings that run long are unproductive and expensive.
- Never give people stuff to read while you are presenting or facilitating the meeting. They will end up halfway listening and halfway reading and lose all focus.
- Never read a lot of material to anyone for any reason.
- Set a protocol that includes the following: no interrupting; you must be recognized to contribute; no talking over people or in side discussions; no looking at your Blackberry; summarize all actions. If you don't have a protocol that sets a performance bar, everyone will make up their own rules.
- If decisions are made, re-state them so everyone understands what is going on. Never assume that everyone heard what you heard.
- If the meeting is about safety or other really important technical material, take the time to ask whether everyone understands or has any questions. Don't assume that silence equals comprehension.
- Watch body language closely. When you or others are talking, take cues from the non-verbal communication of your team.
  - Are people actively listening?
  - Are they looking off in other directions?
  - Are they looking at papers, text messages, or other distractions?

○ Are they leaning back or away from you or the group?

○ Are there side conversations going on? All these are cues that you or the meeting or both are terminally boring or going on too long.

- End the meeting with a summary of all actions decided, including who is going to do what and when.

Running a Productive Jobsite Huddle

In construction there is often a definite lack of communication with field employees and even less with their direct supervisors or foremen. Rarely do field craftspeople have all the necessary information to perform at their highest level from a technical or motivational standpoint. To avoid this problem, I suggest you consider implementing the "jobsite huddle" concept on your projects. A jobsite huddle is pretty much what it sounds like: a short meeting of all hands to review the game plan for the day. It should be no longer than five minutes, and the content might include some of the following:

- The goals or objectives for the day
- The potential obstacles to those goals and strategies to overcome them
- A review of the current project schedule to production
- The opportunity to praise the team or individuals publicly for previous accomplishments
- Reminders on key issues from safety to paperwork to owner interaction
- An opportunity to solicit ideas from the team on a very brief but interactive basis (a key motivator for buy-in)

If a construction foreman does not engage his or her team with information that involves and motivates them, then employees are simply there to perform a job function and earn a paycheck. The jobsite huddle has the potential to engage employees as real team members.

Managing Problems

Time Is Not Your Friend

There is something unpleasant that you are putting off. In reality, you need to do something right now. You are thinking that time might take care of the problem. You are thinking that he, she, or it (as the case may be) will magically be transformed. You are procrastinating. You hope that ignoring the situation will simply make it go away.

Stop bullshitting yourself.

Time is not your friend, and a good leader knows it. Sure, there are times when you need to let something settle down, let tempers cool, let more information come in, or allow for a strategic opportunity to offer itself. I am not talking about any of these situations. I am talking about that thing you know you need to do *now* and yet keep putting off until *later*. Most of the time these situations have to do with *people* issues.

Leadership demands honest assessment of a situation and prompt action. Lots of people will tell you that is how they lead, but they will be lying through their teeth. The truth is that most people do not want to take actions resulting in personal discomfort or conflict. Most managers hold the completely illogical position with respect to people issues that "they will get better." Whatever the problem is, it will not get better on its own. Either you are actively engaged in fixing the problem or it is getting worse. No matter how much you want to ignore it, the consequences will get worse by the day. Classic examples of waiting for change that will never come include:

- The employee you know you need to discipline or fire but never do
- The leader or supervisor under you who is really not ready, capable, or competent (besides, with whom would you replace this person, anyway?)

- The family member, friend, cousin, or long-term employee about whom you think you "can't" do anything
- The terminally late employee (but, hey, it's just a few minutes)
- The great producer who is a cancer in the team
- The employee you would not trust to walk your dog but whom you trust with your clients

Leadership demands brutally honest assessment and immediate action. Don't allow things to accumulate. You cannot lead and manage by looking over your shoulder. If you let things stack up, you can find yourself overwhelmed by the sheer magnitude of actions that need to be taken—not to mention the stress and mental anguish that goes along with the territory. An Alpha Dog takes action now. Faces discomfort. Takes the risk, resolves, and moves on. Want some tips? Ask your family dog.

Your Dog Is a Management Genius: Carpet Surfing

If the previous material went over your head, let me try something a little more direct and crude. If you don't understand the necessity of prompt action, take a clue from your family dog, for he acts like the Harvard MBA he really is.

You ever see a dog with some poop stuck on its butt? What does it do when it discovers this poop? It immediately sits its butt down on your Stainmaster* and scoots all over until it has gotten the poop off. Smart dog. Good dog.

The dog does not over-think the issue. The dog does not stall and pretend. The dog does not rationalize. Your management genius dog understands the following strategic issues better than most leaders and managers:

- Everyone can clearly see it (except you).
- The longer you leave it on your butt, the harder it is to get off.
- You look stupid with it on there.

- You are not fooling anyone.
- There are going to be uncomfortable or embarrassing moments during the removal, but it will be worth it in the end.
- When it's gone, the dog does not think about it any more and happily proceeds to licking a favorite body part.

Your dog is a management genius. Learn from him.

Managing Problems from Your Subordinates

There are five things to review quickly when handling problems brought to you by your employees:

1. Determine whether it is a real problem. Employees often come to their bosses with things that to them appear to be problems but may be excuses to get face time with the boss—venting sessions, micro-detail issues, confusion as to intent, schedule, or something similar. When an employee comes to you with a problem, you need to meet it with patience but also discipline. Train your employees to come to you ready to articulate a problem, both to save you time and to help you determine whether it is a real problem.

2. Do employees come with a solution? Be sure to train them to come prepared to provide options for you to choose from. You are not a dumping ground for problems and issues they are capable of handling. Send them away the first few times until they can present options. Be prepared for an initially negative response but know that the delay will be worth it in the long run.

3. Is an employee jumping the chain of command? Are you making yourself available to people who have others they should go to first? Are you spending time because of personal relationships, your need to feel important, or the job you used to have? Are you picking up slack for someone else who is not doing his or her job or has bad habits?

4. Engage in active listening. Ask questions. Clarify anything that is unclear. Ask employees what they want the outcome to be. You will find it is easier at times to help people find solutions than to take ownership of them yourself.

5. Follow-up plans should be made.

    a. What is the timeframe for the response or solution?

    b. Are you handling the problem? Is the person who brought it to you now handling it?

    c. When will you again discuss the solution or outcome?

    d. How do you leave the meeting and with what agreements?

Bring closure to meetings and make sure to follow-up. Lack of follow-up discourages subordinates from going to their bosses. If they go a couple of times and the results are not positive or clear, they will stop going. Then little problems become big ones that still land on you, just later and in much worse condition.

Managing Problems That Come from Above

When a superior asks you to handle a problem or challenge, he or she should naturally follow the advice outlined above. If a problem is coming down to you, you should do the following:

1. Ask for a specific timeframe for a response. When does the task, problem, research, or report need to be completed? Be specific. A lot of times when the boss asks you to do something, everything else comes to a grinding halt—even if the problem is not an urgent priority.

2. Consider what resources you might need to solve the problem or issue. Don't walk away telling the boss you have it handled and then two days later come back and ask for more help or resources. He or she has already moved on to five or fifty other problems or challenges since then. Now you are pissing him off.

Try to identify what you need on the front end when you take ownership of a problem and ask for it clearly and assertively.

3. Try to identify overlap. Ask if anyone else is also working on the issue. As a boss, sometimes I would have two people working on the same thing without really thinking about it. This situation usually pissed off one or both parties as well as wasted time and resources. I did not do it on purpose; I was simply not managing well. The busier a boss is, the more likely he or she will engage in overlap assignments. Try to determine whether you are coming in on someone else's "thing" and whether a formal assignment is necessary.

Managing Discontent or a Mutiny

There you are, sailing along and everything seems to be going great. Suddenly you turn around and part of your team or crew wants you to walk the plank. Employees are sullen or non-responsive or no longer seem to respect your direction or authority. How does this happen? How do you handle discontent or a mutiny?

Visible discontent or a mutiny is usually the result of a long period of grievances, issues, or neglect. If you are at fault, you need to own it immediately. Don't blame a team that is making you accountable. Don't push back because you've lost your edge or integrity. But there will be other times when discontent will be unnecessarily pushed along and nurtured by someone on your team.

Your first instinct will probably be defensive and angry. You will want to start knocking heads. You may imagine that if you hang someone as an example, everyone else will suddenly see the light. Well, a little ass chewing and minor intimidation might have their place at times, but those are "reactive" rather than "proactive" strategies. These situations don't just develop overnight. You may well have contributed to them, and if you react with a heavy hand, your employees may go haywire.

My best suggestion is to fire all of them. No, just kidding (almost). Intelligence and psychology are your tools here, and you need to understand what has brought you to this point. Sometimes you may be surprised. Little things that have been overlooked can fester and eventually explode. They can be related to your leadership blind spot. They can often be very easily fixed as long as you know what to do. Good leaders know when to use the iron fist and when to use the velvet glove. Make sure you know the root causes before you take any major course of action. Restoring confidence, morale, and a sense of unity can be a critical challenge, and it takes a lot more than a reactive gut-check approach.

Effectively Resolving Conflict

Conflict in the workplace is a given. As in life, at work there are going to be people who don't get along. Conflict needs to be minimized and managed but can never be eliminated—and probably should not be. Conflict can create change. Conflict can challenge assumptions. Conflict can differentiate performance expectations. Conflict also emerges from competition. But despite these benefits it can also be a draining, expensive, and negative influence in the workplace.

If you are engaged in workplace conflict, you need to remember the following:

- You are only capable of controlling your own responses to conflict.
- You are not capable of controlling anyone else.
- Conflict is not always logical.
- Passivity or "waiting for it to go away" is not a constructive approach.
- Storing up frustration or anger will only make it worse when you deal with it.

- Timely response to conflict is important.
- Third parties should only be brought in to facilitate, not to have to listen to or take sides about how one party is right and the other is wrong.

When conflict arises in the workplace, usually one of the parties goes to someone else to share it or to try to get sympathy. Third-party validation of conflict is a coping mechanism that people engage in because they don't know what else to do. Or more likely it is easier to find a willing person to vent to. This is unacceptable and immature behavior for both parties that sets a bad precedent on the jobsite.

Generally, I do not listen to employee complaints about other employees unless they can identify something specific they want as an outcome. I am unwilling to let people vent about others. That gets too close to gossip, and the leader must stay above this. I also don't allow people to get involved as cheerleaders. It seems there is always someone in the workplace everyone goes to with their personal complaints and issues. If you are spending time as a venting destination, you are stealing time and promoting negativity in the workplace. From the first moment you indulge your team by becoming their personal complaint department, you are telling them that it is acceptable behavior to come to a leader this way.

If you yourself do not handle conflict well, then you can expect everyone who works for you to handle it poorly as well. You are the case study they are influenced by every day, and your responses, good or bad, will likely be echoed by them. Be measured, patient, and mature, even when you don't want to be.

When you are attempting to resolve a conflict between people, consider these strategies:

- Examine the conflict root causes not the behaviors. What is the driving reason beneath it? Don't get caught up in the he-said, she-said nature of the conflict.

- Most conflict has underlying behavioral themes that need to be understood before you can get to resolution strategies. These might include:
  1. Competition for position or status
  2. Politics or manipulation
  3. Us vs. Them groups
  4. Passive-aggressive behavior—people unable to communicate issues or frustrations who take it out in other ways that are negative
  5. Competition for resources
  6. Insecurity of one or both parties
  7. Poor communication or listening skills
  8. Incompatible work styles
  9. Breaches of values or integrity

My point is that you cannot resolve conflict by looking at the symptoms. You have to get to and deal with the causes.

Here are some ways I deal with resolution of conflict:

- Ask one or both parties what they want exactly as the final outcome.
- Ask people to identify the "payoff" for a conflict, as in what are they getting out of it since they keep on engaging in it.
- Ask them what they have already done to try to resolve it.
- Ask them what they are willing to do to bring about that result.
- Talk to them about the difference between being liked and respected.
- Talk to them about personalization, how some people bring a defensive or oversensitive nature to the workplace where everything is taken personally.
- Provide them with resources such as books and videos to assist them in developing new strategies.
- Tell them they are both fired unless they start getting along.

Going Beyond the Peace Talks

You will note that what I did not recommend in the previous section is for a leader to sit down regularly with both parties as a mediator. I reserve mediation for very special circumstances. In the rare event that one party is really working at it and the other is not or that the quality, timeliness, or team chemistry is really being severely impacted, then I bring everyone in for an intervention. Under these circumstances I use a different set of messages as follows:

- I expect a 100 percent effort no matter what the job relationships look like.

- I expect mutually respectful treatment and will tolerate no less, no matter who likes or dislikes who.

- I better not hear that they are involving other people in the organization and wasting their time trying to win support.

- I will not wait out someone's willingness to make an effort. Lack of effort in conflict resolution is a matter of stubbornness, immaturity, or fear. All of these are unacceptable. I will help and support someone until he or she demonstrates an unwillingness to cooperate. Unwillingness = unemployment.

- There are consequences. Obviously, it depends on the severity of the conflict, but if I have to be involved, I am going to make sure there is a strong incentive for the parties to commit to some level of resolution.

- I may also assign them a joint project. Sometimes it requires taking their focus off each other and putting it on the work. I would also likely be especially tough on their final work product. Sometimes it is useful to appear as a common foe (for a little while) to both parties while they are recalibrating their relationship.

Finally, there are just some situations that defy resolution. As a leader dealing with conflict, you sometimes need to make hard decisions: to fire someone, to allow low-to-medium-level conflict to exist, to read people the riot act, to wait it out for the short term. I don't like any of these options much, but conflict is a function of the complexity of every person in the workplace, and no leader is good enough to resolve conflict under all circumstances. Sometimes you just have to shake your head and move on.

Dealing with Absenteeism

Absenteeism is usually one of two things: a symptom of other more serious issues the employee is facing or simple lack of self-discipline or motivation. Absenteeism (and the excuses that come with it) can be an indicator of personal problems (drugs, alcohol, divorce, injury, etc.) or something superficial (don't care, lack of pride, don't get big picture, lack of motivation or commitment).

In either case your range of options includes: coaching and counseling, formal warnings, or termination. Make sure you keep accurate records of attendance. Also make sure employees understand the consequences of their actions. And make sure everyone else does too since they are watching you to see what the real policies look like in action.

Handling Tardiness: Twenty Hours Late Per Year

Tardiness is either encouraged or discouraged by the culture you create within a company or on a jobsite. It is human nature to push the envelope of self-comfort, and tardiness is an example of this. Although sometimes it may seem petty, just five minutes a day every day for a year is more than twenty hours in lost time and productivity.

There are five basic strategies for dealing with tardiness:

1. Be very specific about what the expectations are regarding being on time. Let employees know exactly what you expect and what the consequences are going to be for failure to meet those requirements.

2. Abide by those expectations yourself all the time or you will have zero credibility.

3. If any employee has a pattern of tardiness, don't just express irritation. Ask the person what he or she is going to do differently. Make the employee articulate a plan of correction.

4. Apply whatever policy or practice you establish fairly and uniformly. It cannot vary employee to employee or situation to situation. If you send mixed messages, you will get mixed results, and they will be your own fault.

5. Follow through with warnings and discipline. If you do not show people that you are serious, you will experience tardiness "creep." Five minutes late in the morning will become ten; five-minute breaks will become fifteen.

Late arrivals, late breaks, late lunches, or early quits represent time and money. They were not put in the bid to meet the schedule and satisfy the client.

Stamping Out Harassment

Construction as an industry often gives itself permission to be less professional, sensitive, or progressive than many other business sectors. One of these lapses that shows up more than it should is in the area of harassment. In the past, in blue-collar settings, some women and minorities have been the victims of harassment that the perpetrators saw as "just having fun." That kind of "fun" was never in style and is now illegal.

Any form of harassment in the workplace is unacceptable. Gender, race, age, religion, and the like are off-limits for any workplace consideration or judgment. Your organization should have a non-harassment policy. If you have not signed one, ask your boss why not. It can protect both the organization and you personally from any claims by having a formal protocol to follow in the event of harassment. Harassment would include but not be limited to:

- Any form of threatening behavior, either verbal or physical
- Any reference to race, creed, or gender in regards to work or performance
- Any solicitations that lead to discomfort or unwanted attention
- Any sexual, racial, or similar references—including so-called humor, materials, photos, or electronic media—that others find offensive

The courts have a pretty easy way to remember the rules on harassment. It's called the "reasonable person standard." If a reasonable person would consider it harassment, then a court would find for the victim. So be reasonable at all times. Assert immediate leadership pressure on anyone brushing the edges of being unreasonable. And bring down the hammer swiftly on those who are not being reasonable—not only because it is the law or because you are the leader but because it's the right thing to do.

Drugs and Substance Abuse

Drugs and booze in the workplace have become a problematic issue for employers over the years. It is also a problem for frontline supervision because in most instances supervisors are the ones who see the problem and need to know what to do. Here are the key points to remember if you are on the frontlines:

- Most companies now have drug policies or drug testing. Supervisors need to make sure they fully understand both the content and procedures associated with policies and testing.
- All these policies need to be observed in a uniform and fair manner.
- Confidentiality is critical. As a supervisor you are responsible for keeping any information you obtain directly or indirectly absolutely confidential—that is, before, during, or after any employee issues, including discussion of anyone's drug tests or results.

- When to take action is a serious question. Supervisors often have suspicions about employees who may be using drugs on the job. But what is the trigger for referring someone for help or for testing? This is not a subjective question, and if you don't know the answer and are responsible for enacting or enforcing these policies, you need to know. Most every drug or substance abuse policy will have very specific actions spelled out. You need to know what to do based on the circumstances and evidence you have. There is a huge difference between someone coming to work with red eyes and another guy snorting lines off the hood of his truck right in front of you.

- Consistency with local and state laws as well as union agreements is another consideration. If the employees you are supervising are under a labor-management drug/alcohol policy, then you need to follow that protocol; otherwise, you may be compromising both employee rights and employer disciplinary options. Remember that not every union agreement has the same terms and conditions, so don't automatically make that assumption.

F'ed Up and Busted: A Look at Company Culture

Drug and alcohol issues can reveal a lot about an organization's culture. Here's a quick case study concerning this issue: A few years ago I was asked to help out a construction company CEO who received an alarming call from one of his field offices. A call came in from two junior engineers and the superintendent of the project. Their main manager was passed out stone cold drunk on the bathroom floor of the job trailer. They wanted to know what to do. The CEO called me.

I spent some time talking to him about the employee and his relative value to the firm as well as about company policies, values, and culture. Ultimately, the company found an out-treatment program for him, obtained counseling for him and his wife, and helped him out of alcoholism. He is now a very loyal lifetime star for the company because of its compassionate and counter-intuitive approach. But that is not the real story as far as I was concerned.

After it was over, I called the CEO and hammered him. How long had the guys at that field office known? How long did they cover for this guy while he boozed his way through mismanaging people, resources, money, and projects? After some detailed questioning, we found out they had known for more than six months. They had been covering up for him. I laid that on the CEO and his senior leadership as their fault. If the team can't come to you until they run out of both good and bad options, what does that say about your company culture?

What is the real problem here? The fact these young guys did not know better or that they allowed someone to fail because they did not want to rat on the guy? Either one is the wrong answer. The real problem is that the company culture permitted it to happen. Somewhere between that CEO and the field, a new set of rules was applied that did not put the company's interests first, no matter how bad the situation was.

If you want to build a culture of excellence, people have to tell the truth, including giving the bad news immediately. You have to trust people to tell all the truth when it is necessary and then support them even if it is very difficult. You have to be transparent with problems about people and the company so people are willing to come forward. You have to show people that a closed culture is a killer to the people in it.

Strategic Discipline: Giving Warnings

Having handled hundreds of termination cases for contractors over the course of my professional career, I can tell you that most foremen and managers do a poor job of giving under performing employees warnings at work. They just let problems build up until they get sick of them and then angrily fire the person. This approach can create both liabilities and logistical difficulties for an organization. Here are the basics when you have to warn an employee about performance issues:

- Provide a warning when it is warranted. Don't let things slide a few times, because you are only going to undercut the validity of the warning when you finally do give it.
- Provide the warning in a confidential setting.
- Tell the employee exactly what he or she is being warned about.
- Stay specific about the exact reasons and do not get off track.
- State what the expectations are for future performance.
- State what the consequences are for future performance failure.
- State the duration for review of improvement if applicable.
- Ask if the person has questions.
- Ask if the person understands, not if he or she agrees.
- Determine whether you want the warning to be verbal or in writing. Remember that a verbal warning carries much less weight and provides no documentation.
- Be sure that the warnings you are providing are in line with your organization's personnel policy or any applicable union agreements.
- Make sure you are consistent about treating all employees the same when giving warnings on performance.
- Do not provide warnings when you are so angry or frustrated that you cannot clearly concentrate or communicate.
- Have a second party there for documentation purposes if you are concerned about the individual's integrity, stability, or litigiousness.

Flexible Discipline: Cutting Slack

Are employee discipline and treatment always black-and-white issues? No. I'd like to think that every person and situation can be addressed exactly the same way, but that is very unlikely. It can be very difficult to balance the interests of your organization with basic human empathy and compassion. How do you know when to cut slack and when to crack the whip? Have you ever been let off the hook by a cop who could have given you a ticket? Most everyone has at least once.

There are no absolute rules when dealing with people working for you who are having problems. Money problems. Relationship problems. Drug and alcohol problems. Health problems. Attitude problems. If you lead long enough, you will experience them all. And though is it often tempting, you just can't fire everyone with a problem.

Here are some questions that should guide your decisions to cut limited slack in the workplace:

- Can you see light at the end of the tunnel for the person? If so, it may be worth cutting slack.
- Is the person's lack of performance highly visible to others, thus setting a bad example and undermining respect for you?
- If you cut slack for this person, what will others expect as a result?
- Are you cutting slack only because this person is a friend or family member?
- Are you violating serious company policies or values by cutting slack?
- Can you rally the person's team or subordinates to help the person though a bad period?
- Is the person responsive to coaching or efforts to help him or her?

- Are the problems repetitive or chronic?
- Is the slack expected?
- Can a display of your empathy or compassion bond your team tighter or raise people's respect level for you or the organization?
- Can you afford to cut slack from a financial or operational standpoint?

All of these constitute "gray areas" that are not absolute. But using them to process a decision will probably be helpful.

Ten Absolute Rules for Terminations

Terminations are never pleasant and are almost always emotionally charged. In construction, terminations are often delayed or handled poorly for both of these reasons. I have terminated a few people over the years and have handled many termination cases. So let me share with you my ten absolute rules for terminations:

1. Ask yourself whether the punishment fits the crime. Do not overreact. Make sure that whatever action you are taking is uniform and fair and that every employee would be treated the exact same way for the same problem or violation.

2. See if warnings and/or previous documentation exist. Unless it is a serious and gross violation that justifies immediate termination, it is always in the interest of the organization to make sure you have provided the employee with an opportunity to address his or her performance. In this way it is not a surprise and there is no one at fault but the employee. If you blindside someone without any prior warning, the person's response is going to be more emotional and will often lead to additional conflict, grievance, or litigation.

3. Do your homework. Before terminating someone, make sure you have done a proper investigation of all circumstances, issues, and

questions. Make sure you have spoken with any and all persons who might be witnesses in an arbitration or civil case and have obtained their statements or information prior to the termination. Don't try to round up that information after the termination because sometimes people's memories get fuzzy when they don't want to get dragged into workplace conflict and complications.

4. If the employee in question is covered by a union agreement or employment contract, be sure your termination is in compliance with that agreement. If you are not sure, ask early in the process.

5. When terminating an employee, don't make it a long, drawn-out process. Do not get into a debate or argument. Be clear about the reasons. Give the person direction about what is expected immediately following termination. The termination meeting should go like this:

   - Reconfirm that you're on solid ground in discharging the employee.
   - If you do have grounds to discharge, write a termination letter or slip to present to the employee.
   - When the employee arrives, don't beat around the bush.
   - In some cases you might ask the employee whether he or she would prefer to resign rather than be fired.
   - Give the employee the letter or termination slip you've prepared.
   - Finish the meeting.

6. Do not engage with the person emotionally no matter what he or she does or says. Recognize that this can be a life-changing event or at least a very painful one. Responses can range from shock to hostility to resigned acceptance. Don't be surprised and don't buy into anyone's response. Also, don't try to "make it all better" because you can't.

7. Have all details wrapped up. Have paychecks ready. Request truck keys right then. Have health or pension information or other necessary data available. Don't give someone a reason to come back.

8. Allow the person to save face (unless it is a very gross violation and you want him or her out immediately). Do the firing either at lunch or at the end of the day so the person does not have to face or interact with other employees. If the person has tools, office materials, or other things he or she has to collect, make sure you have the ability to assist the person in collecting those materials immediately. The person should not be returning to retrieve anything for any reason.

9. If you are concerned for any reason about the stability or litigiousness of the employee, have another manager present for documentation and/or safety purposes.

10. Explain the termination to the other employees but with a minimum of detail. Do not go into details about anything that was done or said. Do not bad mouth the employee. Do not encourage gossip or speculation. Do not vent. Do not revisit. Once it is done leave it alone and move on.

Handling Depression in the Workplace

Depression in the workplace is estimated to cost businesses in the U.S. $44 billion in reduced productivity per year. This is in addition to the toll it takes on families and personal lives. Still think it is not a problem? Well, more than twenty million people are currently on some form of medication for depression, anxiety, or similar problem in the U.S. and Canada. It is an absolute guarantee that you know people who are dealing with these kinds of problems (or who have chosen not to).

Leaders need to be aware of depression and its consequences. It is a serious medical problem that has significant workplace impacts.

Twice in my career I have had key employees slip over the edge into depression. Both situations proved to be very difficult and complicated for them and me.

Just last month a friend and very successful business leader called to tell me he is a wreck. He has been depressed and in denial. His marriage is on the rocks, and he has almost destroyed his family and himself. He had to spend a week at my house with my family taking care of him. It might seem surprising that a guy with money and success would have anything to be depressed about, but that is the reality of life. He put his feelings and emotions on hold. He tried to wait out his personal baggage. He crashed and burned. What you see on the outside often has nothing to do with what people are dealing with on the inside. He trusted me because he had no one else he could turn to who would not judge him or think he was weak.

This is the first and most important thing: Take it seriously, and don't be judgmental. Depression is not something that is an inherent weakness in the individual; it is a medical issue. Especially with guys, any issues like this can be seen in terms of an individual not being strong or self-sufficient. As a result, a lot of people will bottle up their feelings until the symptoms become so acute that you are wondering what the hell is wrong with Mike or Tom or Sandy; and by that time it has already done significant damage.

Here are three ideas you might consider for assisting a peer or subordinate with whom you have a good relationship. Remember, depression is a very personal issue.

- Discuss it in the context of work performance. If someone is not performing, ask some leading questions to try to get the person to address the subject. I have also given a couple of people a day or two off to come back to me with a performance improvement plan that includes self-focus.
- Help the person see the logic of taking action. I simply tell people, "If your car was running on five cylinders, what would you do?

See a mechanic. If your taxes were a mess and you were getting audited, what would you do? See a CPA. If your knee was hurting from a fall on your mountain bike, what would you do? See an orthopedic doctor. So if someone is bummed out and unhappy, what should he do? Take action."

- Suggest counseling: At different times in my leadership I have nudged more than a few of my employees toward counseling. That might seem to cross the line dividing personal matters from business, but I cannot afford to have extremely unhappy people in my organization. They under perform. They impact others significantly. And they cannot help it. Sitting around waiting for them to crash makes no business sense to me. Two people had to leave my organization because they were unwilling to confront their issues. I still wonder if I could have helped more.

Saving the Drowning Man

We have covered more than a few personal problems your employees will challenge you with. Sometimes it can feel like you are a therapist, parole officer, priest, or father figure. It takes some basic compassion to be a good leader. But you can take it too far. You can get into the idea that you can save people as their boss or supervisor. Some leaders really thrive on helping those with tough personal challenges—these drowning men of the workplace. What are the telling signs of drowning men?

- The subordinate or coworker who is "having personal issues" and missing a lot of time
- The employee whose performance has dropped off dramatically in a very short time span
- The person who has a serious life drama that spills over into the workplace regularly
- The person with a visible drinking or drug habit or similar affliction

- The guy who can't be reached regularly and has vague excuses of where he's been
- The person who explodes with rage, dissolves into tears, or says nothing to anybody for no apparent reasons
- The person with financial or relationship challenges who looks to others to solve them

I am not saying that a good leader leaves people to drown without compassion, but you have to remember that if you take time to give these people extra attention, the rest of your team will notice. A drowning person also usually (out of panic) drags others under who try to save him or her.

If you allow drowning people to flounder without either a solution or consequences, the rest of your team will resent you and them both. Your kindness or desire to help someone can also be seen as favoritism. Your allowance and tolerance can be seen as setting double standards for performance. The simple rule has to be to treat everyone as an individual, but at the same time do not vary your standards and expectations too far just because someone has serious "issues." Make sure also that your team supports your efforts when you are spending that extra time with a troubled soul or drowning man. If you don't, you risk alienating your team or crew with little likelihood of success.

Locked and Loaded: No Uzi in the Job Trailer

It is hard for me to believe that this even needs to be covered in a book on construction management and leadership, but the subject is ripe for review. In my more than twenty years I have known at least a dozen companies that have had serious violence in the workplace. These situations ranged from bloody fistfights in the shop to an Uzi being sprayed in a job trailer. One only needs to pick up a paper on a monthly basis to see some new story of a person bringing frustration or mental illness to the workplace with accompanying violence.

I even have personal experience with this. In one instance an apparently disturbed employee in a conflict I was handling for a contractor appeared to be getting ready to shoot me. As he reached for what we thought was his gun, everyone around me dived, ducked, and covered. I turned sideways, walked backward, and prayed. The situation was resolved without major incident, but I was teased for about five years for the look on my face. It wasn't that funny for me. I learned a valuable lesson. When people are pissed off and/or unbalanced, they can do some crazy things. Thus, as a leader responsible for the safety and well-being of your team or organization, you need to be thinking ahead.

Here are some basics regarding violence on the project or in the office:

- The company must have a zero-tolerance policy for any form of violence in the workplace.
- The company must have a zero-tolerance policy for the bringing of any firearms, weapons, or similar items onto company property or into company vehicles.
- Employees must be comfortable reporting what they perceive to be threatening behavior toward themselves or others.
- Company office employees should report any phone threats or altercations to senior management.
- Employees acting in an erratic manner need to be interviewed early. Don't write off such behavior as someone just having had a bad week or month.
- Terminations or layoffs can trigger these types of behaviors. Be aware of this fact and plan accordingly with employees. Do not put administrative or financial staff in the position of having to interact with terminated or angry ex-employees.
- Any actual situation that arises needs to be handled by law enforcement. Coach your supervisors or crews not to engage

someone and offer themselves as targets. Coach your office staff on how to lock down the office quickly and efficiently.

Although it may seem like overkill (no pun intended), most schools and universities and many businesses actually hold drills along these lines these days. Sad but true. It is therefore important to have some idea of how to handle violence in the workplace before rather than after it occurs.

Managing for Safety Excellence

Taking responsibility for safety in the workplace is a very important part of construction supervision. Now and then you hear on the news about someone getting injured, burned, or killed in the workplace. To most construction guys on the job, it just seems so far away—as in, that could never happen to me or those on my team. But for millions on the jobsite, dangers are a daily reality that are often not fully understood or appreciated.

Old-school thinking was that safety was not macho. Safety was a hassle. Safety was something the guys upstairs cared about. I was a victim of that kind of thinking way back when, and my situation resembled the stories below. They are all true. They are from a period when I put myself through school, working construction in downtown San Francisco. The company is (deservedly) long out of business.

I hefted the sawzall up again and began cutting. The pipe wrapping exploded in a cloud of white dust. Sweating in the crawl space, in my paper dust mask, I cut those pipes for weeks as we did the demo and conversion on that old tenement hotel. And at the end of those days, I looked like Casper the Ghost, covered head to toe in white powder. Just another construction guy doing his job. Except that dust I was wearing and breathing was asbestos. Know what? If someone had told me that, I probably would have kept doing it anyway....

I dipped the steel wool in a canister of industrial JASCO paint stripper. Thick and poisonous. Used a respirator with two-month-old filters or foam dust masks. Stripping three coats of paint off fifty old hardwood doors. Stuff stank up an entire floor of the job. Just another construction guy doing his job. I knew it couldn't be good for me, but I was young and immortal anyway....

In a hurry I climbed aboard that second-to-the-top step on the ladder, the one that says "This Is Not a Step." I was stripping lath off a ceiling that was just out of reach. Oops. With a twelve foot fall I only bounced once, but the crew got a laugh out of it. Just another construction guy doing his job. Setting a great example of production before protection. Boss didn't care. Foreman didn't care. I didn't know better. Old-school thinking about jobsite safety was dumb as hell and twice as dangerous.

Later in my career, as part of my job, I ended up teaching job-site safety classes to thousands of rank-and-file construction guys. I wondered how many guys had been just like me. At the beginning of each class I would ask how many guys had been on a jobsite on which someone had been killed or seriously injured. A large majority of hands went up. I would then go around the room and make every guy tell his story. By the time we were done, I had every one of them locked in to what I was teaching. Personal responsibility went from far away to up close and personal. Now, you would think that all these guys who had seen the brutal reality of unsafe practices would have great track records. Not even close.

After a few hours of instruction I would do another exercise. I had everyone write down the most unsafe thing they ever did on the jobsite and put it into a box during lunch. No names. No companies. Just their stories. Then I would finish with the worst of the worst. I would then select the Idiot of the Class.

What came out of that box were stories of stupidity, recklessness, and barely avoided death and destruction. It was hard to believe. Worse, there were a lot of supervisors in the classes. The topics of the stories ranged from heights to depths to high voltage. From safety guards removed to hazardous chemicals and atmospheres to riding in buckets and down wires. It went on and on.

I would read the very worst out of that box to the class, and everyone would shake their heads and sometimes laugh. Finally, I would select the Idiot of the Class, and everyone would cheer. The guy selected would usually say, "Hey, that was me." Then I would tell them stories from my personal box.

I told them about the project I was on in which four guys were burned to death. The project I was on where a fall resulted in rebar sticking through a guy's leg. A guy who broke his neck. A guy whose legs were crushed. A guy who was killed when he rolled his backhoe. The guys that got killed in traffic. A guy electrocuted on a 12KV line. A guy who drowned in a pipe. A guy who cut off three fingers. They stopped laughing.

Safety is not about policies and rules. Safety is about shaping decisions and behaviors. How do you shape these behaviors? Not by getting people to read and sign a hundred-page safety policy manual. How it gets done is like this:

- Training is the foundation: You cannot change behavior unless people know what the right behavior looks like. And more importantly the "why" behind it.
- No exceptions or compromise: The prima donna guy who thinks he is too good for the rules goes home.
- Mutual accountability: Everyone watches out for everyone else all the time.
- Goal orientation: Everyone should know how many days since the last accident occurred. Everyone should know the workers' compensation losses and ratios and how much time was lost.

Why? Because you have to use some kind of measurements to motivate people. Just telling them "Be safe" doesn't do it. You have to have something to point at that indicates success or failure.

- Engagement is vital: Almost every employer has safety meetings. Are they just a dull administrative mandatory function in which someone reads off a paper? Or are they interactive sessions that engage everyone on the crew for suggestions, problem solving, and proactive strategy?
- Rewards and consequences: If you want to shape behavior, you have to have a stick and a carrot.
- Understand that safety is good business and adds to the bottom line for everyone.

The Idiot of the Class exercise shows that almost everyone has compromised a critical value system of safety in the workplace. Even knowing the consequences, people still did it. Exposing themselves to danger daily or maybe only for a few seconds in an entire year, the risk seems inconsequential until fate steps in with injury or death. The "It can't happen to me" factor is very high, especially where male macho construction behaviors encourage high-risk activity. Thus, the shaping of norms and behaviors needs to come from the supervisory personnel, especially foremen, in word and action, all the time.

CHAPTER
FIVE

Alpha
Motivator

"If your actions inspire others to dream more, learn more, do more and become more, you are a leader."

—JOHN QUINCY ADAMS

Motivation and the Pinnacle of Success

Mount Rainier is a 14,000+ foot volcano perpetually sheathed in glacier ice. It is magnificent, awe-inspiring, and unforgiving. In a recent icefall, our guide broke his nose, jaw, cheek, palate…and knocked out seven teeth. Many climbers have died. It is said to be the toughest endurance climb in the lower 48. Our climb starts at midnight, and I'm feeling the wind chill. It's 20 below.

It is easy to talk a good motivational game. The world is full of people who give me their "I always wanted to, I thought about it, I ought to" speeches. I feel for them because they don't get it. It's really not money, power, or what others think that opens us to living fully. Truly living is about taking actions that provide the self-respect, esteem, and fulfillment that comes with knowing we are living up to our potential. It is harnessing our motivational capacity. It is too easy to pretend, to others and ourselves. Thus, testing for the truth has a price.

Black ink night. Harness, helmet, ice ax, headlamp, solitude. Thin air and a silent rope. My world is a two-foot circle of light and one more step. The hours pass. Kicking in each step. Winds stagger us. Ice crystals sting. With motivation the body can only follow the mind.

Lots of people and businesses are much the same. "We're making money. "We must be good." " I've got my journeyman card." "No one's complaining, so why worry?" This type of ignorance may be short-lived bliss. Simply put, if you are not absolutely committed to your personal and professional potential, you are not only missing an essential competitive strategy, you are shorting yourself and those around you. But how to know, if you don't really push your motivational limits?

> *We reach 11,500 feet, the Ingraham Glacier headwall. In 1981 eleven people died there in an icefall. Their bodies were never recovered. More than one thousand feet of 60 degree ice. It will be at least three hours non-stop. Tiny headlamps of other teams dot the hulking black shape far above us. The wind shrieks. Right there a group of climbers quit; they simply unclip from the team ropes. Though having traveled from Illinois, Florida, Montana, all over the States, they do not Pass Go. No attempt. Perceived motivational limit reached. All done.*
>
> *The phrase "pinnacle of success" implies that the top is a small place, accessed only by arduous trial. This is true. But where you start matters. For a year I have trained from 4 A.M. to 6 A.M. six days a week. Carrying a pack. Lifting. Running. Biking. Waiting for today. I did not start climbing this son of a bitch today. I started climbing it a year ago.*
>
> *On this headwall I am sucking freezing thin air. My glove is off for a minute to secure gear. Three of my fingers lose all feeling. I bang them against my thigh each step. For an hour. The team in front of us is stalled. We cannot stop behind them or we will freeze and fail. We must abandon our switchback approach and go four hundred feet straight up and around. I can't do this, I think....*

The lessons of the mountain apply to the challenges ahead for construction. I believe that the purity of the challenge is there and that those willing to commit will see the reward. I believe that it is the arduous circumstance that bonds people to achieve more. Perhaps I am a lone voice, but those with a belief in "good enough" or "the status quo" need to think about hanging it up for good.

I make the top of the headwall but can't talk. Then another thousand feet up. We cross a crevasse hundreds of feet deep. On a ladder. We jump over another dark, bottomless crack. Our water bottles are frozen. Chapstick breaks off. We do not ask how far. I really do not want to know anymore. I just know that quitting is no longer an option.

Legitimate achievement earns respect. And that sums up my personal way of life. Associate with a group of highly motivated individuals who will not quit on each other. Live for clear and measurable goals that most think unattainable or would not even think to set in the first place. Share credit and acknowledgment of success. And plan enthusiastically for the next objective. It is a model that presses the capacity of both the individual and the team. We all know that our greatest test, that of success as individuals, a company, and an industry always lies just ahead. I guess I'm just stubborn, but in reflection of a life well lived or job taken on, I'll take exhausted exhilaration or flat-out failure over safe complacency every time.

I can see the summit. It seems miles away. One step every ten seconds. Finally…reaching the top, I collapse on all fours. No joy, but a sense of self-mastery. For the first time in hours I turn to look down. I see the sun is rising above clouds two miles below. The sight is worth it all. Through doubt and beyond perceived limits, the test is complete. At last we exchange grim smiles and agree that the climb was the hardest thing any of us has ever done. Eight to ten more hours of descent now waits, but the truths we have learned about ourselves will be with us forever.

Winning Heads and Hearts

What Motivates You Does Not Motivate Others

Since most people look at the world thorough a filter of their own thoughts, feelings, and experiences, we sometimes expect others to see it just the same way. When it is up to you to motivate your team, though, this assumption can be a big obstacle to enhanced team performance. You have to remember that what motivates you does not automatically motivate others.

Yes, I know that this fact is a major inconvenience. If only everyone just did their damn job like you do and didn't require all this effort to find out what makes them tick. But what makes them tick is as individual as they are. And to apply your own motivation criteria or simply to guess is poor leadership practice.

Winning the 25-50 Motivation Challenge

In a survey by William M. Mercer Inc., 25 percent of workers said they were capable of doing 50 percent more work. On average they reported that they could likely do 26 percent more work. That indicates a lot of lost potential and productivity. That is a hell of a lot of money on the table. What is going on here?

You ask average workers how their days are going, and they are going to start telling you how *busy* they are. But busy is not necessarily productive. Activity and outcomes are often not aligned. This study indicates that no matter how "busy" they are, they are not producing at their potential—and more than that, *they know it*.

Here are the top three reasons for underachievement given by more than a third of the survey respondents:

1. *Lack of rewards for a good performance*

If you get nothing else out of this book, you by now realize that this responsibility falls directly on you as leader, supervisor, or manager. It does not have to be dollars. It has to be a reward. From word to gesture to material actions, rewards and recognition are your most powerful motivators, and at least a quarter of your workforce is likely starving for them and in return does not reach their potential.

2. ***Lack of involvement in decision making***

Again, this is a frequent theme of the book. Asking people for input creates buy-in. Buy-in creates loyalty and commitment. And all of this boosts productivity and output.

3. ***Lack of opportunity for advancement***

People want to know the direction of their career paths. If you have the opportunity to coach people on this subject, you are killing two birds with one stone. You are giving them something to shoot for in the future and simultaneously motivating them to perform better today. Don't wait for them to ask about it; make it a part of your dialogue with your people. Recapture that 26 percent. It's just waiting for you. Cha-ching.

Understanding the Roots of Motivation

High achievers, in my experience, are not always as motivated externally as they are internally. What I mean is that people have very personal reasons for high-achievement behaviors. Some important ones include:

- Fear of failure
- Need for recognition or validation
- Proving something to one's parent
- Competing with a sibling
- Driving personal self-esteem from emotional "baggage"
- Proving self-worth

These are not quite as positive as one would hope and are a lot more complex than just paying people more. So, if there are hidden motivators that most of us can tap into, how do we get to these?

As we covered in chapter 2, I consider "self-education" the best approach to getting people motivated. It relies on them understanding more about themselves and their own potential. Sometimes it is not as much educating them on what they *are* but more on what they *are not*, which is done by removing their performance obstacles, helping them chuck personal baggage, modifying their self-limiting beliefs, and providing them with an opportunity to expand their perception of themselves. It is about getting your employees to face that same "mirror" we talked about in chapter 2. Your lessons of self-knowledge can be passed down to them.

This is not the common approach to construction leadership and management. It's easy to yell. It is more time intensive and sometimes more confrontational to make people face their own potential. But once you have tapped that reservoir of self-motivation, they can operate at a high level while seeking superstar status with little more than ongoing maintenance.

Motivating with Your History and Stories

For the last ten thousand years an oral tradition of telling stories was the primary way information was passed down from generation to generation. These stories helped newer generations understand the history of those who came before and shaped the values and culture of the family or tribe. These stories were the foundation of individual identity and group unity. The power of stories can still be harnessed and used in today's world and especially in the workplace. To motivate and engage your team, I strongly encourage you to tell your stories.

Here are stories that most every leader or manager might find useful to tell:

- The Organization's Story: This helps employees understand the organization's history and traditions. To create a relationship beyond the paycheck, a company needs to tell its story to connect the new to the old and to preserve good traditions in the face of rapid and often necessary change.

- The How-I-Got-Here Story: This helps people place you and your accomplishments in context. Employees may only know you as the boss and not understand the difficult and lengthy road you traveled to arrive there.

- Your Major F-Up Story: This is a personal story of failure shared to humanize you. It is a parable of sorts as it is designed to teach employees how not to fail and also to show that no one is above failure. It provides a unique opportunity to show some vulnerability and humility. It can also be a story of encouragement or redemption.

- Your Parables of Performance: These are examples, both good and bad, of people and performance in the workplace. What they did to inspire. What they did that hurt the team or employment. Stories of rapid rise or failure with swift and terrible justice.

- Personal Real-Life Stories: If you are a trusted leader, at some points your employees will come to you asking for personal advice. Or perhaps you will see them struggling with personal challenges. I think that this is also a good time to tell them a personal story, if you think the content can help them work out their own issues. I do not think it is a great idea for managers and leaders to become too enmeshed with their employees' personal lives, but in many cases they simply may have no one else to turn to. Think of stories from your life you might be willing to share that can provide others with a roadmap to resolving their own problems.

Embracing Failure (Yours and Others')

To motivate others, you need to learn to love (or at least accept) failure. Not in a way where you look forward to it, but love it with a strategic familiarity that will tell you about yourself, your subordinates, and your organization. Some individuals and organizations do not deal with failure well. They do not optimize the event. They do not use it as a platform for additional motivation and systemic improvement. This is a critical mistake. Here are ten ways failure can serve a leader and organization:

1. Failure as a learning event. Analyze "*what* went wrong and how do we avoid doing it ever again" instead of "*who* screwed up and what is going to happen to that person as a result."

2. Failure as a systems checkup. At least half of failures are systemic, meaning that the real problem in an individual's performance can be tracked back to the system in which he or she operates. It is easier to bawl out the person than to analyze the system, but that won't resolve underlying issues. Ask: "What is the root cause of this failure? And what systems address the issue?"

3. Failure as a test of poise and control.

4. Failure as an assessment of risk-taking behavior (good and bad) in the organization.

5. Failure as a method of assessing the judgment of your subordinates.

6. Failure as an opportunity to promote accountability. Ask what employees can and will do to fix any given problem. In some cases also ask what they think the consequence for their failure should be.

7. Failure as a method of building scar tissue and mental toughness.

8. Failure as a method of assessing motivation. Does a failing employee come to you disappointed and self-critical or with a cover-my-ass attitude and an excuse?

9. Failure as a "notch-taker-downer." Some people (including some of you reading this) think they are infallible. Humility sometimes needs to be stuffed down your throat by Mr. Failure.

10. Failure as a training opportunity. Your employees will learn more from watching you deal with their failures in a calm, focused, and results-oriented manner than you can imagine.

Motivational States of Being: Can, Can't, or Won't

In the process of evaluating the base motivation of a person it is easy to overanalyze. As such, here is a very simple way to assess an individual's motivational "state of being" by categorizing him or her according to one of these three profiles:

- The Motivational State of "Can": The person is performing and is clearly capable of performing at or above expectation levels. He or she is highly self-motivated and operates well with guidance, adequate resources, and a clear timetable.

- The Motivational State of "Can't": The person lacks skills, resources, confidence, and/or guidance. He or she is not automatically incapable or a lost cause but needs additional training or handholding. Management needs to diagnose the barriers to success. Self-evaluation or assessment can help bring clarity to an employee's view of obstacles. This person is worthy of a remedial plan with a strict timetable for improvement.

- The State of "Won't": The person may or may not have skills and capabilities for high performance. He or she demonstrates an inability to self-motivate or exercise self-discipline, general attitude problems, and may have difficulties with prioritization, responsibility, or authority. This kind of employee is generally not worth the time necessary to shape or modify his or her behavior, no matter the skill level.

Master Motivator and Mentor

Using the Big Three (Dependable) Motivators

There are three dependable motivators in the workplace. If you are not using them, then it is very likely that your team and organization are not operating with the greatest effectiveness. The top three you can put to work tomorrow are the following:

1. ***Praise and Recognition:*** Praise and recognition are the number one motivators in the workplace. Though this should seem obvious, I am always surprised by their absence in construction. It is not unusual for less than ten percent of the construction leaders in my training programs to report using praise and recognition on a consistent basis. What are the barriers to the other ninety percent of construction leaders? Why are they not using the number one most powerful motivator? Here are some excuses:

   - People should do their jobs without getting their asses kissed.

   - I was not taught that way (especially common statement from foremen).

   - Being complimentary is not the way of the jobsite.

   - We tell people what they do wrong, not what they've done right.

   - If I praise them, they might get a big head.

   - If I praise them, they might want more money or perks.

   - Fill in your blank_____.

     Praise and recognition profoundly influence performance. They simply cannot be ignored in the name of outdated construction traditions.

2. ***Participation in Decision Making:*** Participation in decision making is the second most powerful (and underutilized) motivator in the construction workplace. Throughout this book there are multiple examples of the positive impact of obtaining

employee buy-in. Employees are more motivated if they share ownership in ideas and initiatives. A top leader gives them ownership. A top leader gives them a voice. A top leader asks for their input, ideas, and contributions.

3. *Compensation:* There is still a place for material rewards in the compensation formula. People want to know they are valued materially and financially. Compensation is in some ways a reflection of self-worth. Money by itself may not be a top motivator, but if you under compensate an individual, you will certainly impact both his or her motivation and retention.

Motivation: Ten High-Performance Affirmations

If you want to know whether your employees are highly motivated, then help them to sign off on the following ten affirmations. As you will note, they are not complicated but when combined can make a significant impact on performance:

1. I know what is expected of me at work.
2. I have the tools and materials I need to do my work at my highest degree of productivity.
3. I have an opportunity to do what I do best at work.
4. My supervisor cares about me as a person.
5. My opinions count.
6. I receive praise and recognition when I do well.
7. My organization provides me with the opportunity to learn and grow.
8. I am proud that I work for the organization.
9. I receive regular feedback or coaching on my performance.
10. At work I understand both short- and long-term goals and my role in achieving them.

If a manager or leader has employees who answer yes to most of these, it is very likely he or she has a highly motivated and high-performing team. This material can also help facilitate an employee performance evaluation.

Motivating Using Goals and Measures

Who would watch the NFL if no score was kept? What if your kids had no report card to bring home? The very basic concept here is that goals and measurement always impact performance. If you use goals and measurements to benchmark performance, then you are in a better position to show your employees their progress. Goal accomplishment is very satisfying for individuals or a team. Work activity without an identified end in mind becomes mindless.

A good foreman sets goals and reports progress on a daily basis. A good CEO sets annual goals and puts together systems to track progress. Goals are tangible. They make the effort of the individual, team, or organization meaningful. Measures such as time, hours, incidents, schedule, and so forth all can be powerful motivators if used properly. Possible reportable measures you can consider using in your organization might include:

- Jobs that make money as opposed to those that lose it
- The percentage of projects from repeat clients
- The percentage of any project completed against the schedule
- Cost to estimate data
- Units of production per day and per employee
- Safety loss ratios or lost days
- New clients secured per year
- Customer satisfaction ratings
- Total hours worked in a year-to-year comparison
- Total employees worked in a year-to-year comparison
- The organization's total year-to-year revenue
- The total revenue generated per employee
- The number of quality "call-backs" per month or in a year-to-year comparison

Many contractors hold most of their data such as this very close (or they don't track it at all). In the interests of trying to keep it confidential, they lose the potential motivational impact on their entire management chain. I have seen dozens of highly successful contractors share their data with very good results. So every organizational leader has to ask: Do we measure success in our organization or on our crew? Do we communicate it? Do we analyze it with our management team? Do our employees respond to it? And if not, why not and what opportunities are we missing?

The Motivator: And Grown Men Cried

Jim Dixon is my brother-in-law and a general foreman. He runs large projects for a major national contractor. His jobs make money. Jim teaches Bible study. Jim has volunteered at jails to help rehab prisoners. Jim doesn't drink or smoke. Jim makes grown men cry.

Jim was a key plastering supervisor on the construction of a major stadium a couple of years ago. His job was the number one project in the nation for his company. Profit. Productivity. Quality. And they were very appreciative. They gave him a big bonus. Like over $25,000. On the same crew but different job, two of his key guys told him they did not want to come back to work for him. Said he pushed them too hard. One of them started crying. Let's go back to the cash bonus. What would you do with a $25,000 bonus? I know he always wanted a Harley. I figured he would finally get it. He didn't; he gave $20,000 of it to his crew.

Now, I would not have done it. I guess I'm simply too selfish. But here is a profile in true Alpha leadership. He pushes so hard that his crew cries. He runs the number one job in the nation. And then he gives the majority of the credit and money to the guys that made it possible. Where do you think his guys would follow him? Anywhere.

P.S. He bought the Harley with what was left and his own money.

De-Motivation: Perfectionism and 98 Percent vs. 2 Percent

Are you a perfectionist? Have you ever worked for a perfectionist? Not good. Not fun. Let's take a quick look at perfectionism and its impact on team motivation.

Is a project or program a success if 98 percent of it exceeds all expectations? Or does that other two percent always merit mention, review, or emphasis? I guess there is a difference if you are doing heart transplants versus painting a fence. But sometimes perfectionism can sorely impact team morale. Don't be a leader who always focuses on that 2 percent. It's like when you were a kid and busted your ass at school to get six As, but all your dad could talk about was the one C you got.

If you are a perfectionist, there are other challenges. You probably nitpick people. You often take far too long to complete tasks. And if there is even one thing mildly wrong with your work product, you are disappointed and self-critical, even to the point of being distracted from the big picture. Perfectionism is a control issue that can make people miss the 98 percent and only focus on the 2 percent. It is not a true leadership trait.

Motivation Killer: "You're Not Paid to Think"

In the field construction culture there is no phrase more stupid and short-sighted than "you're not paid to think." And yet nearly all construction field hands in the U.S. and Canada tell me that they have heard it dozens of times on the jobsite, especially when they were apprentices. Tell me what other business sector commonly communicates the value of dumbing down the workforce? What is a construction leader or manager actually saying when he or she uses this idiotic phrase with a key employee or new apprentice?

- Your ideas have no value.
- You are nothing but brute labor.
- We are not interested in innovation or change.

- I am in charge, and don't forget it.
- We don't care about you.
- I don't know how to motivate, manage, or lead you.

The truth of today's industry is that thinking is what people are paid to do. We need to turn out "knowledge workers," not just "skilled tradesmen." Again, if you can't reach employees' heads and hearts before their hands, a productivity loss is going to occur.

"You're not paid to think" is an authoritarian statement that represents poor training on the part of senior management. The fact that nearly every field craft person still hears it is an indicator of outdated values in the construction workplace. It is bad enough that the young employees coming into our industry have to experience it. But the real question is why would an industry allow a mindset to exist on the jobsite that costs, say, a billion dollars a year in lost productivity, profits, and market share? Let's kill "You're not paid to think" once and for all.

Motivating and Training Your Replacement

Any good organization tries to promote from within. This is a long-term success strategy. So if key leaders are not developing their own replacements, that says a lot about their organization's lack of vision. It also means they have significant barriers to future growth with built-in delays of time, training, and resources.

For an organization to grow and succeed, people need to move up quickly. Every manager and leader needs to help in this regard and not worry about their own jobs. Those who help then move up. Those who don't clearly don't understand the dynamics of organizational success. Drive this message down the ranks to the very last guy on the jobsite. There are still many field leaders uncomfortable with this concept who, in order to protect their own jobs, restrict the ability of the organization to grow and prosper.

Motivation, Communication, and the Ten Percent Rule

It is estimated that people only remember ten percent of what they hear. Why is this important? Well, when you consider that most of the teaching and direction given in the office or on the jobsite is verbal, the ten percent rule is pretty damn important. So remember:

- When you talk to your employee for five minutes, he or she might only retain around a minute's worth of the conversation.
- When instructing someone, it is important to be brief and clear.
- If you remember the Ten Percent Rule, you won't be frustrated when it seems like employees never listen to you.
- The more you talk, the less content people are able to remember.
- You might need to provide supplemental learning tools.

When you are trying to motivate or teach someone verbally, you have to remember that ten percent is a relatively small amount to really sink in. So, if you can say it in ten words instead of fifty, you have a much better chance of getting your message across. Other ways you can improve your listeners' rate of retention include:

- Telling stories so that an imprint of an event is illustrated as part of your communication
- Supplementing your verbal communication with visual aids
- Showing and telling, not just telling

Teaching and Learning: The Rules of Retention

Keep in mind the previously noted Ten Percent Rule when teaching any task; in addition, let me suggest these additional points as the Rules of Retention:

- Always tell employees the "why" of a task. Why is it being done? Why is it important? What are the consequences of it not being done or it being done poorly?
- Speak clearly and don't rush.
- Do not just tell workers how if you can show them at the same time.

- If written or visual cues or information can be provided, retention rates will go up three-fold.
- Have employees perform a task while you monitor it and provide feedback rather than doing it yourself.
- If time permits, have employees repeat a task or the instruction immediately after it has been completed.
- Ask if anyone has any questions.
- Ask workers to confirm they fully understand the task, process, and desired outcome.
- Ask people test questions if you think they are unwilling to admit they really don't get something.

By the way, for all you house-on-fire Alpha personalities, here are some things you should not do when teaching an employee:

- Be impatient or distracted while giving instructions
- Tell employees only the outcome you want and then send them away
- Jump in and out of instructing, thereby breaking up the sequence of task instruction
- Take over for someone who is struggling, thus getting the task done but not teaching it and having to teach it again, at a different time, making for a greater time investment
- Yell at people while they are learning—it makes them nervous, and they tend to perform poorly

Finding and Developing Coffin on the Back Guys

I was talking to a very successful contractor a long time ago. He started off dirt poor and moved from Ireland to Canada and then on to the U.S. His personal net worth now is probably in excess of $50 million. Not that money is everything, but I tend to pay attention to people with a rags-to-riches background. Plus, he's just a great guy. He said to me, "Mark, to make it in business, you got to have some 'coffin on the back guys.'" I told him I'd never heard that term before.

He told me a story to illustrate his meaning: "Way back in the last Iran-Iraq war, some of the soldiers would build their coffins at home before they went into battle. Then they would carry them on their backs out to the fight. Now *that*, Mark, is what I call commitment. That's what you need in business, a few of them."

At the time the story seemed morbid and a little weird. But the more I thought about it, the more I could appreciate what he was saying. You don't bully people into a commitment like that. You don't "manage" people into a sacrifice like that. No, you obtain a level of buy-in and loyalty that transcend the ordinary. Most successful organizations have a few "coffin on the back guys," and many times they are not the top company leaders but guys out on the foreman's frontline. As hard as it may be, finding and developing a few of these guys should be a leader priority. They will do anything for you and the company out of loyalty and obligation, but you will have to earn those things first.

The Price of a Ten Percenter

In most construction workplaces about ten percent of workers are under performing. They lack the proper skills, attitudes or behaviors. These are not my off-the-cuff estimates; these numbers come from tens of thousands of people I have asked about poor performance in my presentations across the U.S. and Canada. Ten percent seems too high a failure rate for a professional industry like ours.

I do not often meet foremen or managers who intervene or fire someone in this ten percent category in a timely manner. Foremen and leaders need to understand clearly the cost of the under performer, the ten percent at the very bottom of your workforce when it comes to skills, attitudes, and work ethic.

The price of this ten percent will include:

- Impact on schedule, production, and profit: The estimator did not put these workers in his bid.

- Impact on new employees: The ten percent is showing new employees from their first day of employment that marginal performance is tolerated, which has a profound effect on new employee work ethic, commitment, morale, pride, and teamwork. The new employee does not have to be there long to determine that the manager in charge is not relating performance to compensation or job responsibilities. They are impacted, tainted, and can be ruined as a result.

- Company cohesion, identity, and pride: Tolerating low performers sends a message to everyone in the field about company values and expectations. Part of a company's identity and brand is the way people act in accordance with those values and expectations. Any compromise has a ripple effect that goes a long way.

- Impact on the client: The construction end user paying the bills can usually tell the ten percent from the rest of the workforce. By appearance, pace of work, demeanor, quality, or something similar, a ten percenter will show clients they are not getting their money's worth.

More often than not, a foreman or manager struggles with decisions about the ten percenters without thinking about the "hidden costs." Make sure your organization does not "price around" this problem without considering the impacts listed above each and every time.

Who Let the Dogs Out? You Did

How much sympathy would you have for a guy who complains about his own body odor? Or maybe someone who goes on about weight problems while chowing down two Big Macs and super-size fries? Or the guy who tells you with a straight face that it pisses him off that he is balding but the reason is he pulls his own hair out?

Simply put, you'd tell them to do something different, wouldn't you? You'd tell them to take some responsibility, show some backbone, and stop the complaining. Why is it, then, that I hear so much complaining from construction leaders about the lack of quality, commitment, and skill of the construction guys on the average jobsite? How did that ten percent we covered previously get by for all these years?

I know most construction supervisors are busy—not just busy, but slammed. More work than time. More promises to be honored to owners and developers. More projects to man-up and more money to be chased. When it gets really busy, sometimes performance standards can be compromised. We sometimes reach a stage at top peak employment that I call the "send-me-a warm-body" jobsite hiring practice. And worse, this is inevitably when the friend, brother-in-law, superintendent's kid, or dude-who-walks-your-cousin's-dog gets a referral. Unqualified. Unprepared. Unskilled. Unacceptable.

The construction industry is fighting against an on-going erosion in the skills, attitudes, and behaviors of rank-and-file workers. You will not find anyone who thinks the general talent pool is on an upswing. So what is the point? The contractor is always the "sole judge of qualifications." And who stands in the contractor's shoes on the job? The foreman. What this means is that the ultimate screen and filter is possibly you. What this means is that the quality of the overall workforce depends entirely on field supervision to eliminate the ten percent of workers who lack the skills, attitudes, or behaviors necessary to compete. What this means is that bitching about the quality of workers solves no problems and is pretty damn hypocritical if we are not getting our part of the job done.

There are solutions, however. Here are just a few:

- Do not refer someone to employment in construction based on a relationship unless you are sure he or she is suited for this industry. Pre-assess attitude, work ethic, transportation, skills, personality, willingness to learn, and more. Don't drain our competitive edge by trying to do someone a favor.

- Filter the existing workforce. Every contractor has the right to reject or terminate employees who are unqualified. Most union agreements now allow contractors to write letters so that unions can re-assess these employees and even restrict or eliminate their dispatch eligibility. What do contractors do now? RIF. Reduction in force. Make that guy someone else's headache. Spin him, replace him, park him where he can't do a lot of damage, and move on. The foreman won't play the heavy or the company does not care enough to document a poor performer. How does this serve our competitive interests?

- Build a reputation for zero tolerance. The industry has to have no place to hide. When any new guy gets to a job, he should be assessed immediately. If you don't cut it, you're history. Every job, every time. Guess what? Lousy hands will soon find this industry less accommodating of their marginal efforts.

In the next ten years the baby boomers are going to start retiring. Hundreds of thousands of contractor employees over the age of forty-five are going to start moving out. And these are the moneymakers, the old-school work ethic guys. Many of them are irreplaceable. So it is the responsibility—no, the *obligation*—of every contractor, foreman, and lead man in this industry to make damn sure new hands who come onto the modern jobsite are worth that $40 to $65+ total package they are likely getting.

Who let the dogs out? We did. And it's long overdue that we do something about it.

The Come-to-Jesus Speech

There will come a moment when you have to confront an employee, when his or her future employment is on the line. The challenge is to motivate the person to embrace different behaviors immediately or lose the job. My employees call my approach Mark's "Come-to-Jesus" (CTJ) speech. The theme is very clear. It is about choices.

The CTJ is something many managers skip. Instead of adopting a productive approach, they instead yell or berate. They usually end up firing the people in question. Instead of leaping to drastic measures, my CTJ is about giving employees final choices about performance and commitment, responsibility and growth, sacrifice, and future opportunities. I deliver it with full eye contact. There is no room for misunderstanding. It is a threat and a promise. Sometimes it is delivered calmly. Sometimes I can run a little hot.

If you try a CTJ speech, do not be surprised by people's responses. They may become defensive. They may become hostile. They may be remorseful. They may be very quiet. They will be emotional. I have been cursed out. I have seen men cry. I have had people walk out right then and there. I have also seen people truly get it and embrace the message. A few people who have had the CTJ have become positive contributors to our company, and several have even attained "superstar" status. Some tell me that the "Come-to-Jesus" meeting was a painful but transformational moment in their lives.

CTJ summary: Don't beat around the bush when someone's livelihood is on the line. Don't be incomplete or vague. Don't yell and scream and rant and rave without a message. Don't leave any room for non-comprehension. At the conclusion ask the person whether he or she fully understands. Give the person a chance to ask any questions. Employees deserve the opportunity to fully evaluate their final choices. But this is their last opportunity to choose well, and they have to know that too.

Leveraging Adversity

You've heard the phrase, "When times get tough, the tough get going." Or maybe they just give up in despair and roll over. What people do in tough circumstances has a lot to do with leadership. Adversity can be a remarkable opportunity to bond people together, or it can be the catalyst for chaos and conflict. When your organization or the people in it are facing adversity, what do they most really want and need from their leaders?

- Reassurance that the leader has a plan
- Consistent communication about what is going on
- A confident and generally optimistic leader
- Honesty and transparency
- Empathy and understanding
- Poise under tough conditions

No matter what you are really thinking, you cannot let a negative response to adversity show to a great degree with your people. They are going to take their cues directly from your behavior. If you get negative, so will they. If you become a blamer, count on the same from them. If you lose your confidence and poise, they will too.

Adversity is the time to ask more of people and make them see the value of their contributions. It is an opportunity for people to stretch, but they are going to want to know that it is somehow worth it. The leader is the one who has to communicate that value to them.

The Death of Mentoring? (Not on Our Watch)

If you are like me, you did not get to where you are in life without someone mentoring you. I think of mentoring as someone taking a personal interest—someone who's really understanding and extending themselves above and beyond a basic relationship—someone with whom a real connection of trust, communication, and mutual benefit can be made. Mentoring is a very powerful motivational and developmental tool that regularly plays a key role in most of our personal and professional lives.

Mentoring now seems at risk in our industry. I was unaware of the decline until quite recently, but the proof now seems overwhelming. I have had the privilege of speaking to tens of thousands of construction leaders in the past few years. The audiences vary: contractors, project managers, CEOs, union leaders, engineers, foremen, and many journeymen. I ask these audiences the same question: "How many of you have had someone mentor you for success?" Every time almost ninety-five percent of the more experienced guys raise their hands. But when I ask this follow-up question, the problem becomes clear: "How many of you now are taking a personal interest in and mentoring someone in your company or industry?" Now very few hands go up—probably less than twenty percent. That weak response is startling, and it is truly in our interests to find out why it exists.

I asked guys who don't mentor anyone why, and the responses were as follows:

- The kids today are not willing to be mentored.
- It is not worth the time to invest in them.
- I don't have the personal time to do it; we are moving too fast.
- I just don't think about it that much.

On the other hand, when I ask young guys why they think they cannot obtain mentoring, they say:

- The older guys don't want to teach us because we are a threat to their jobs.
- They think mentoring is yelling at us or toughening us up instead of showing us how to succeed in the work and the industry.
- No one has offered, and I don't know how to find or ask someone.

There has never been a time in our industry when mentoring has had more value. With the impact of changing generations on competition, stability, and talent development, mentoring is a strategic necessity. And despite excellent training and strong contractor leadership, no one factor has more upside potential for influencing performance than mentoring does.

I would like to suggest four strategies that the industry should adopt to ensure mentoring does occur:

1. All contractors should go to their supervisors and ask them who they are mentoring. All construction supervisors in the U.S. and Canada should be actively developing at least one or two guys as a regular part of their jobs.

2. All managers, leaders, and supervisors need to understand the purpose and benefits of mentoring.

3. All leaders should tie the message of mentoring to the long-term benefits that serve everyone in the industry in order to break down any old-school thinking about not teaching the new guys out of fear or insecurity.

4. All young people coming up need to know to find a mentor. They need to know how to find someone who is willing to invest in them.

I am personally mentoring five young guys right now. I meet with them or call them monthly. I hear about their lives, work, marriages, dreams, problems, and more. Mostly, I listen. When I do speak, I know it really matters. I see them changing their lives right in front of me. My payoff is the realization that I have done the right thing for the right reason for the right person.

As you go on with your business of the day today, ask yourself what valuable life lessons you have to share that others could profit from hearing. Or, if you are a young guy or gal on the way up, know that there is some experienced person willing to take you on if you show the proper level of commitment. Mentors are waiting out there for you right now. Let us not let the great tradition of mentoring die.

Seven and a Half Questions to Ask a Mentor

A mentor's honest feedback and insight can very valuable. But some young people don't know how to enter into a "real" conversation about important issues. A lot of people just wait for the mentor to initiate the subject matter. The cause of this lack of initiative can be intimidation or simply not knowing what to ask.

So here are 7.5 questions to create valuable learning content for anyone wanting a mentor. They will lead to an interesting exchange for the mentor as well:

1. What is the one thing you do that creates the most opportunities for your organization?

2. What motivates you most, and how do you best motivate others?

3. How does age play into leadership?

4. What are the personal characteristics that most successful people you know possess? What common traits do you find in people who don't advance?

5. Can you tell me about a time when you faced a huge challenge or failure and what you did or learned?

6. What one thing should I be working on right now?

7. What is the best advice you can give me?

½. If you could be an animal, which one would you be? (Um, no, let's *not* use that one....)

Mentoring is the last and final gift a leader gives to his employees, his organization, and industry. In it is a distillation of his or her experience and advice. These questions only skim the surface of the potential benefits mentoring can provide to a young person today. I sincerely hope you will take the time to help someone else obtain the rewards and accomplishments that this industry has provided to you.

CHAPTER
SIX

Words to Live and Lead By

 # Honesty

Why It's Important

Honesty is the foundation of trust upon which relationships are built. Honesty is the cornerstone of integrity, which is the desired value system for every successful individual and business. In the absence of honesty, any substitute will kill morale, unity, momentum, and belief. The more honest you are, the more likely people will listen to you, respect you, and do what you ask, request, or command.

What It Looks Like

Truth telling in all forms. No omissions. No "white lies." Timely, relevant, and straight-up communication about what needs to be said or done.

What It Should Feel Like

Freeing. Uncomfortable. Liberating. Awkward. Frustrating. Surprising.

Leading with Honesty

Monitor the frequency, manner, and strategy of your lying. Stop rationalizing untruth. Ask yourself what you are giving up along with giving up the truth. Experiment with painful truth telling. Trust yourself and others to accept the truth.

Toughness

Why It's Important

Leadership is a test of toughness. Competitors, employees, vendors, allies, and enemies all will generally silently assess you for your toughness. In response, you don't have to act like a tough guy; you just have to project strength, determination, and resolve in a clear and unequivocal manner that leaves no doubt about where you stand. Your manner should also give people second thoughts about messing with you.

What It Looks Like

It is the look in the eye and not the size of the muscles. Often it is quiet.

What It Should Feel Like

You know yourself. You know your capacity. You will not back down from your principles and values. You can endure more than most. You project it. You can see its impact on others. They see it in you.

Leading with Toughness

Toughness is a quality that can be rough or refined. It can be callused hands or fire in the eye. It is something that people recognize not because you are loud but because they just get it. You lead, they follow. No questions asked. Toughness breeds the same in others.

# Focus and Concentration

Why They're Important

Focus and concentration provide a laser-like burst of energy for high-value returns. In world where multitasking is considered the norm, focus and concentration are undervalued. Attention spans are growing shorter in our culture. Technology stimulates and distracts moment to moment, and focus and concentration can be lost. The result may be the loss of singular momentum for projects and individual efforts.

What They Look Like

Doing one thing at a time. Not inviting or allowing interruptions in the form of phone calls, email, texting, music, or external stimuli. Doing things or approaching them in a sequence with a plan that is time efficient.

What They Should Feel Like

Highly satisfactory. Visible progress in the moment. Frustrating. Boring. Unfamiliar.

Leading with Focus and Concentration

Focus and concentration move individual projects and initiatives along much faster. Concentration improves productivity and adds to your ability to address details. Concentration moderates procrastination. It also shows younger people, who may be used to constant technology monitoring, that uninterrupted activity is of great value in the workplace.

Self-Discipline

Why It's Important

Self-disciple is the most visible criterion your team will use to evaluate your ability to lead. Your failure to exercise self-discipline will detract from their respect for you and their willingness to follow you. Self-discipline breeds the same in others. It is a very difficult trait to exercise for nearly everyone in at least some aspect of life.

What It Looks Like

Doing the hard thing consistently even when you really don't want to. Doing it without complaint or compromise. Doing your best without an audience.

What It Should Feel Like

Proud. Painful. Often on the edge of compromise.

Leading with Self-Discipline

Concentrate on visible examples of self-discipline. Acknowledge areas in which you are not showing your best side in this regard and stop ignoring them. Your team isn't.

# Patience

Why It's Important

Strategy is not always best served by urgent action. The foundation of accomplishment is understanding timing. Patience is not always a matter of delays. Patience is not always a virtue either. But if you have to choose between haste and patience, with anything of value on the line, patience often provides the best alternative.

What It Looks Like

Calm. Observant. Poised. Ready.

What It Should Feel Like

Easy. Like time is standing still. Effortless. Or, instead, like your nails are getting pulled out. Trying to hold back while every molecule in your being is screaming to "go for it" now.

Leading with Patience

Force yourself to wait. Fight the power of impulse. Don't press others with your impatience if it is not in the service of outcomes. Control your personal need to act in sacrifice for a better outcome. Center yourself.

Humor

Why It's Important

Humor releases stress. Humor is a tool. Humor is a state of connection. Humor used at the right time can make or break a relationship or business deal.

What It Looks Like

Making people happy. A method of communication. A key part of camaraderie.

What It Should Feel Like

Great. People laugh because it's a natural reaction.

Leading with Humor

The leader shows the team what level of humor works. Humor at your own expense pays. Humor at the expense of others is not humor; it is humiliation. Humor at times of difficulty soothes. Humor as a method of connection can bond. Humorless people rarely make good leaders. If you spend forty to fifty hours a week for thirty years at work, you better have some humor in there.

Courage

Why It's Important

Leadership requires risk taking at a much higher threshold than that of an ordinary employee. The manner in which risk is handled is determined by the courage of the leader. There is a difference between a bold lean-into-it leader approach and a lets-try-it-but-cover-our-asses manner. That difference is courage. Organizations thrive or fail based on their assessment and response to risk. Leaders must have a superior capacity to accept risk based on courage.

What It Looks Like

Committed decision making. Zero waffling. Not much second-guessing. No scapegoating. Acceptance of risk. Unruffled and unflappable. 007.

What It Should Feel Like

Paralyzing. Empowering. Ordinary. Exhilarating.

Leading with Courage

Courage is not an inherent and static quality in us. We can grow in courage by exercising it. By accepting risk and the consequences of failure we often grow in courage and confidence. Accept the discomfort and move ahead. Courage is not the absence of fear; it is action in the face of it.

Empathy and Compassion

Why They're Important

Empathy allows you to stand in the shoes of others. Without empathy, a person is solely focused on his or her own viewpoint and feelings. Compassion is human kindness in action. What is more important than that? Leading with empathy and compassion breeds tremendous loyalty and personal commitment.

What They Look Like

Empathy and compassion look like understanding, sincere, and caring behaviors toward others at appropriate times. They are not signs of weakness (especially in guys) but signs of being a secure, centered, and solid person.

What They Should Feel Like

Fulfilling. Heartfelt. Emotional. Real.

Leading with Empathy and Compassion

Show personal regard for those around you, and show sincere care for others. Get over any personal issues or obstacles that make it hard to exercise empathy or show compassion.

 # Initiative

Why It's Important

Initiative is the signal flare of leadership. Those who take initiative earn leadership opportunities. Initiative is about doing, not asking or waiting. Initiative is about confidence. You think you can, so you do. You are not passive. You don't overanalyze. You start the ball rolling when others do not or cannot, and things get done.

What It Looks Like

Jumping in. Deciding to act. Moving to the next logical action without being instructed. Taking ownership. Stepping up.

What It Should Feel Like

Natural. Fun. Scary. Empowering.

Leading with Initiative

You can't make it without initiative. Embrace action now. Use your creative momentum. Don't second-guess yourself out of the running. Show others that taking initiative has rewards. Create an environment of positive motion and emotion.

The Final Word

"It is time for a new generation of leadership, to cope with new problems and new opportunities. There is a new world to be won."

—JOHN FITZGERALD KENNEDY

Within these pages I have tried to plant the seeds of knowledge and inspiration. The question now is whether you are ready to take the initiative and act. If nothing else I have tried to show you that the opportunity to lead never ends and that your personal efforts can have profound effects on others.

In every facet of our lives we have the opportunity to lead others to better outcomes. If we do so in a manner that reaches and inspires others, we set an example for those who will follow us. I have no doubt that some readers of this book will go on to become some of the greatest builders and constructors in the history of North America. But it is also important to remember that it is only through the mentoring of and sincere caring for others that we fulfill our destiny as people.

It has been my privilege to serve you within these pages. Now go out and fulfill your Alpha destiny. I have every confidence you can and will succeed.

About the Author

Mark Breslin is the fourth generation of a construction family. His great-grandfather, grandfather, and step-father were all contractors. Mark started his working career in the field.

He has served as the CEO of the Engineering and Utility Contractors Association, one of the largest and most innovative contractor organizations in the Western U.S. for over 25 years. The association represents hundreds of contractors performing billions of dollars in projects annually. Mark became the chief executive at age 26.

He is noted as the number one speaker in the nation on construction leadership, strategy and labor-management relations. As a strategist, speaker and author he has addressed more than 150,000 business, labor and construction-owner leaders. He also speaks to tens of thousands of field craftsmen and apprentices across the U.S. and Canada annually.

Mark graduated from San Francisco State University with a degree in Industrial Design. He has since taught at both Golden Gate and Sonoma State University. He lives in northern California with his wife Susan and their three kids. Real life passions include expedition and adventure travel. Recent challenges include trekking the Sahara, paddle rafting the Grand Canyon, hiking to Everest Base Camp and raising three teenagers.

Resources
www.breslin.biz

Leadership Assessment Tools (on-line)
Everything DiSC® Management™ Profile & Everything DiSC® Workplace™ Profile

Two highly effective and proven assessment tools for managers and workers to better understand their own potential.

Assisting foremen, superintendents, project managers, estimators and all senior managers better understand their management style, communication and tendencies. Valuable insights can be realized from a clear examination of what works, what doesn't and how to adapt to continue to succeed personally and professionally. A great organizational investment in individual leader and manager development. (1/2 hour online / 1 hour to evaluate results)

Leadership Training Programs
Mark Breslin's "Alpha Leadership"

A transformational training program designed for leaders and potential leaders in all construction related organizations. Meant to remove obstacles to personal change and provide tools for immediate leadership improvement and performance, this program has been used to improve results for leading national organizations as well as small enterprises. Proven and dynamic, it is a necessary step for many in construction who want to professionalize their methods and improve the performance of their teams and organizations. (7-8 hours)

Improve Individual and Organizational Performanc

CHECK **www.breslin.biz** OR ORDER HERE

Quantity	Title	Price ea.	Sales tax–Calif residents only	TOTAL DUE
LEADERSHIP DEVELOPMENT				
	NEW! Alpha Dog (book)	$19.95	1.66 ea.	
	Leadership Assessment Tools	online		
APPRENTICESHIP AND RANK & FILE: materials and media				
	Survival of the Fittest (book)	$19.95	1.66 ea.	
	NEW! La supervivencia del más apto (book)	$19.95	1.66 ea.	
	Survival of the Fittest Workbook and Discussion Guide	$9.95	.83 ea.	
	Survival of the Fittest Apprentice and Training Instructor's Guide	$29.95	2.49 ea.	
	Survival of the Fittest Training Pack (book, workbook, instructor's guide, and DVD sampling, plus the Rank & File Education Series DVDs)	$393.00	32.62 ea.	
	Survival of the Fittest audio CD (2-CD set)	$24.95	2.07 ea.	
	Survival of the Fittest DVD	$149.95	12.45 ea.	
	Survival of the Fittest T-shirt: M L XL XXL	$19.95	1.66 ea.	
	Survival of the Fittest Poster: "50 Strategies for Jobsite Success"	$9.95	.83 ea.	
	Rank & File Education Series: The Breslin Business Plan DVDs (2)	$249.00	20.67 ea.	
	NEW! Million Dollar Blue Collar (book)	$19.95	1.66 ea.	
	SHIPPING: $3.95 per item*	_____ items x $3.95 =		
	TOTAL:			

*FREE SHIPPING when ordering 50 items or more.
Canadian orders must be accompanied by a postal money order in U.S. funds. Allow 15 days for delivery.
Quantity discounts available • Call 925-705-7662

My check or money order for $_____ is enclosed.

Name_____ Phone _____

Organization_____ E-mail _____

Address _____

City/State/Zip _____

Please make your check payable and return to: **Breslin Strategies, Inc.**
7172 Regional Street #430 • Dublin, CA 94568

or to charge your purchase visit **www.breslin.biz**
or call **925-705-7662** • *fax* **925-705-7426**